ARABIC
FOR
BEGINNERS

with a Guide to Arabic Writing

T0204805

HIPPOCRENE LANGUAGE STUDIES

اللُّغَةُ الْعَرَبِيَّةُ لِلْمُبْتَدِئِينَ

ARABIC FOR BEGINNERS

With a Guide to Arabic Writing

Dr. Syed Ali

HIPPOCRENE BOOKS
New York

INTRODUCTION

Arabic language has to-day assumed the status of an International language. With the emergence of sovereign Arab States, in Asia and Africa, exercising considerable influence in the political and economic spheres, interest is evinced in this language by people living in the four corners of the world. It is unique that Arabic, though a classical language, is good enough for an age whose scientific and political vocabulary is increasingly expanding. Time has not driven it into oblivion as it has done in the case of many a mighty tongue, nor has it undergone any drastic changes during the fourteen centuries and more of its glorious existence. On the other hand it has revitalised itself and become more popular with the passage of time and has attained a singular status which very few classical languages command.

As Philip K. Hitti has remarked: "For many centuries in the Middle Ages it (Arabic) was the language of learning and culture and progressive thought throughout the civilised world. Between the ninth and the twelfth centuries more works, philosophical, medical, historical, religious, astronomical and geographical, were produced through the medium of Arabic than through any other tongue". The European languages are indebted to Arabic for part of their vocabulary, idiom and style. The Oxford English Dictionary reveals the fact that a vast number of English words are of Arabic origin. Its alphabet has been adopted by Persian, Pushtu, Urdu, Sindhi, Turkish, Malay and several other oriental languages.

This volume introduces Arabic to those who wish to learn it through the English medium. This book does not pretend to cover all the finer points of this language nor does it deal with the principles of grammar exhaustively. Most of the lessons have as their heading a grammatical term. The vocabulary - lists of these lessons include the words used in the illustrative text and the model sentences. In these lists, the plural form of nouns is indicated following a dash and the imperfect forms of verbs are shown along with the verbs in the past tense.

Translation of one language into another always gives rise to certain difficulties arising out of the distinctive thought forms and cultural patterns. Literal translation is often unidiomatic. I have tried to bring the translations as close to the originals as possible, without violating the norms of either of these languages. Indicating a vowel mark in the Arabic text leads to some printing problems; hence these have been used very sparingly.

In this edition some essays and poems by eminent writers and thinkers of the Arab world have been added. The student is advised to read Arabic newspapers and journals in order to keep himself abreast with the latest trends in Arabic literature. It is by no means an easy task to attain mastery over Arabic for those who live in a non-Arab environment, but dedication and sustained efforts do produce results.

وما توفيقى إلا بالله عليه توكلت وإليه أنيب

Syed Ali

4, Begum Sahib St.,
Royapettah, Madras - India

CONTENTS المحتـويـات

THE ALPHABET حروف الهجاء

خ ك ح ḥ ج j ث t ت t ب b ا ā

ص ṣ ش sh س s ز z ر r ذ d̲ د d

ق q ف f غ ḡ ع a̒ ظ ẓ ط ṭ ض ḍ

ء a ي y و w ه h ن n م m ل l ك k

Arabic, like Hebrew, Persian and Urdu, is written and read from right to left.* The Arabic alphabet consists of twenty-eight letters. A letter is a conventional mark to express a sound. Most of the letters take different shapes while constituting the first letter of a word, the last letter of a word or while occurring in between. Some letters which are Identical in form are distinguished from one another in writing by the aid of the small dots called "diacritical points" نقطة "Nuqta".

Name of the letter	Arabic Consonants		Phonetic symbol
alif	ا	الف	ā
bä	ب	باء	b
tä	ت	تاء	t

*While practising writing of this alphabet, always write from right to left, i.e. contrary to the habit you have developed while writing English.

Name of the letter	Arabic Consonants		Phonetic Symbol
t̠ä	ث	ثاء	t̠
jim	ج	جيم	j
ḥä	ح	حاء	ḥ
k̠ä	خ	خاء	k̠
däl	د	دال	d
d̠äl	ذ	ذال	d̠
rä	ر	راء	r
zä or zay	ز	زاء	z
sīn	س	سين	s
shīn	ش	شين	sh
ṣäd	ص	صاد	ṣ
ḍäd	ض	ضاد	ḍ
ṭä	ط	طاء	ṭ
ẓä	ظ	ظاء	ẓ
äyn	ع	عين	ä
ḡäyn	غ	غين	ḡ
fa	ف	فاء	f
qäf	ق	قاف	q
käf	ك	كاف	k
läm	ل	لام	l

Name of the letter	Arabic Consonants		Phonetic Symbol
mīm	م	ميم	m
nūn	ن	نون	n
hā	ـه	هاء	h
wāw	و	واو	w
yā	ى	ياء	y
hamza	ء ـ أ	همزة	a

There are some Arabic consonants which have no equivalents in the English alphabet.

The first letter of the Arabic alphabet i.e. ‏ا‏ (alif) is considered as consonant when it carries the Arabic symbol ‏أ‏ (hamza), otherwise it is considered as long vowel. The symbol used to indicate ‏أ‏ (hamza) in this book is "a".

Similarly ḥ ح k ك k̠ خ à ع ḡ غ have no equivalents in the English alphabet. Books of foreign origin have explained at length how the pronunciation of these letters is articulated by twisting the tongue in more than one way. But we have avoided this exercise. Instead of using symbols which could be better understood by academicians and experts of the phonetic system, we have used the familiar English letters with dots and strokes attached to them.

There are letters which may be supposed to convey the same sound, but in fact should be distinctly pronounced. Readers are advised to take care to distinctly pronounce each of the letters of the Arabic alphabet from the start with the help of their instructors. For example ت ث ط should be pronounced distinctly, hence the symbols used for these letters in this book are t, ṭ, ṭ, respectively. Likewise ح ḥ and هـ h س s and خ ص ṣ ك

and ق q and ز z and ظ ẓ,أ a and ع à have their distinct pronunciation

The letter ض (its phonetic symbol in this book is ḍ) is peculiar to
Arabic language. The Arabs call their language "the language of ض"
لغة الضاد presumably because they deny to non-Arabs the ability to
pronounce this consonant.

Some letters of the Arabic alphabet look similar in shape but are
distinguished from one another by the position of small dots "diacritical
points". For example ب ت ث have the same shape, but ب has one dot
below, ت and ث have two and three dots on the top respectively.

ج j ح ḥ and خ ḵ are differentiated from one another by the
position of the dot or the absence of it. Same is the case with د d and
ذ ḍ, ر r and ز z, س s and ش sh, ص ṣ and ض ḍ, ط ṭ and ظ ẓ
and ع à and غ ḡ. Letter ى y is written with two dots below or
without dots.

The letter ت t when used as a feminine ending of nouns and
adjectives is shaped thus ة. Observe this change at the end of the
following noun and adjective تلميذة a girl student جميلة beautiful.

The letter ه h is written as ه : ـه (without dots) when suffixed to nouns
e.g. كتابه kitaabuhu his book

VOWELS اَلْحَرَكات

DIPHTHONG, NUNATION, TASHDEED

The Arabic language had originally no signs for the short vowels. When the Arabic language was learnt by the non-Arabs and when the verses of the Quran were read incorrectly these signs came to be used by the Arabs.

Vowels are usually not indicated in Arabic books, journals or in any written matter, unless when the correct pronunciation of a word is to be made sure. A person who knows Arabic grammar can read correctly any Arabic passage without the help of vowel signs forming part of the text, but a beginner very much needs them.

Every consonant in vocalised Arabic text is provided with a vowel sign (sometimes indicated and often omitted in writing). In the Arabic language a vowel is called حَرَكة "haraka" *movement*. And a consonant with a vowel sign is called مُتحرِك "Mutaharrik" *moved*. If a consonant is without a vowel sign, it is called سا كِن "Säkin" *resting*.

There are three short vowels in the Arabic language. Unlike vowels in English, they are indicated by strokes.

1. اَلْفَتْحَةُ FATHAH (a) ــَ is a small diagonal stroke above a consonant . it is identical with vowel "a" in the English word "man" e.g. تَ Ta, جَ Ja, فَ Fa.

2. الضَّمّةُ DAMMAH (u) ــُ a small و "waw" above a consonant. It is identical with vowel "u" in the English word "bull" e.g. تُ Tu, جُ Ju, فُ Fu.

3. اَلْكَسْرَةُ KASRAH (i) ــِ a samll diagonal stroke under a consonant, it is identical with "i" in the English word "finish" e.g. تِ ti جِ ji, فِ fi, رِ ri, لِ li, مِ mi.

Read each of these consonants once with Fathah ˚ second time with Dammah ُ and a third time with Kasrah ِ

Example:‒ 1. بَ Ba, 2. بُ Bu, 3. بِ Bi.

اُ بُ تِ ثِ جِ جِ حُ خِ خِ دِ ذُ ذِ رُ زِ سُ شُ صُ ضُ

طُ ظُ عُ غِ فُ قِ قُ كِ لُ مُ نِ هُ وُ ئِ

LONG VOWELS AND DIPHTHONG

Three of the consonants ى و ا which are described by the grammarians as "**الحروف العلة**" "Al huruf al illah" *weak or irregular letters* are used for lengthening the vowels.

ا for ä,   ى for i and ai.   و for ü and au.

e.g.: را rä,   فى fi,   كَىْ kai, ذُوْ du, لَوْ lau.

"ا" corresponds to ˚ "ى" corresponds to ِ and "و" corresponds to ُ. Therefore "ا" is called "**اخت الفتحة**." *the sister of fathah* "ى" "**اخت الكسرة**" *the sister of kasrah;* and "و" "**اخت الضمة**" *the sister of dammah.* Thus نَهارُ "nahärun" as opposed to نَهَرَ "nahara"; جُوْدُ "judun" as opposed to جَوَدَ "jawada" and صَدِيْقُ "sadequn" as opposed to صَدَقَ "sadaqa".

When the weak letters are used as lengtheners they do not admit any vowel sign.

"Fatha" ˚ before "ى" and "و" form the diphthongs ai and au. e.g. رَيْبُ raibun *doubt* مَوْجُ maujun *wave.*

Here some Arabic words are written, with the component letters shown separately, and with the vowel marks indicated. This is for the beginners. Remember that if an Arabic word consists of two, three or more letters, all these are written together. (Lesson 3 deals with this subject.)

تَ رَ كَ	فَ هِ مَ	كَ تَ بَ	رَ كِ بَ	وَ صَ لَ
taraka	fahima	kataba	rakiba	wasala
to leave	to understand	to write	to ride	to connect

رَ زَ قَ	نَ صَ رَ	ذَ هَـ بَ	لَ ع بَ	وَ زَ نَ
razaqa	nasara	dahaba	laa'iba	wazana
to provide	to help	to go	to play	to weigh

ضَ رَ بَ	فَ تَ حَ	سَ كَ نَ	كَ رُ مَ	سَ م عَ
daraba	fataha	sakana	karuma	sami'a
to hit	to open	to dwell	to be noble	to hear

شَ رِ بَ	أَ كَ لَ	بَ حَ ثَ	لَ بِ سَ	تَ ع بَ
shariba	akala	bahata	labisa	taa'iba
to drink	to eat	to search	to wear	to work hard

NUNATION التَّنْوِيْنُ

Nouns and Adjectives, when indefinite, the vowel signs are written double e.g. ٌ ً ٍ. In such a case the pronunciation of the word changes. Letter بَ with one "Fathah" is pronounced ba. But the same بً with double "Fathan" is pronounced as ban. Likewise تً tan, جً jan, فً fan. Letter بُ with one "Dammah" is pronounced bu. But the same بٌ with double "Dammah" is pronounced as bun. Thus ثٌ tun, جٌ jun فٌ fun. Letter بِ with one "Kasrah" is pronounced as bin. Likewise تٍ tin, جٍ jin, فٍ fin. This sound, which is not rendered in writing is the so called "nunation".

The sound produced as a result of double vowel signs ٌ ٍ ً on a consonant is called تنوين "Nunation", i.e. though ن is not written it is pronounced.

NOTE:— A word with the definite article ال will not accept "nunation".

In the following, each alphabet is written with double Fathah , ً, double Dammah ٌ and double Kasrah ٍ, read them aloud.

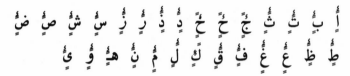

أً بٍ تٌ ثٍ جً حٌ خً دٌ ذٍ رٌ زٍ سٌ شٍ صٌ ضٌ

طٍ ظٌ عٍ غٌ فٌ قٍ كٌ لٍ مٍ نٌ هٌ وٌ ئٍ

SOME EXAMPLES :

أُ سْ رَ ةٌ	أَ بٌ	أُ مٌّ	اِ بْ نٌ	بِ نْ تٌ
usratun	abun	ummun	ibnun	bintun
family	*father*	*mother*	*son*	*daughter*

أَ خٌ	أُ خْ تٌ	جَ دٌّ	زَ وْ جٌ	زَ وْ جَ ةٌ
akun	uktun	jaddun	zaujun	zaujatun
brother	*sister*	*grand-father*	*husband*	*wife*

ABSENCE OF VOWEL السكونُ

When a consonant is without any vowel mark it is called ساكن "Sakin" *Resting*, and the sign used to indicate this is ْ a small circle placed over the quiescent consonant. When one consonant in a word is with the vowel sign and the following letter is ساكن "Sakin" the two letters would form a syllable, i.e. they would be read together and thus produce a joint sound.

SOME EXAMPLES:

مِنْ   لَ مْ   هَـ لْ   دَ عْ   هَ بْ   خُ ذْ   قُ مْ   كَ مْ

min	lam	hal	da'	hab	kud	qum	kam
from	*no*	*is?*	*let*	*give*	*take*	*stand*	*how much*

فِ ئ   لَ أ   مَ أ   لَ وْ   كَ ئ   قُ لْ   كُ نْ   بَ لْ

fi	lä	mä	lau	kai	qul	kun	bal
in	*no*	*what*	*if*	*so that*	*say*	*be*	*but*

The following words consist of three letters but two syllables. In دَ رْ سُ darsun *lesson* دَ رْ are combined and their joint sound is added to the last letter, سـ.

نَ فْ سُ   فَ وْ قَ   حَ مْ دُ   خَ مْ سُ   دَ أ رُ   وَ زْ نُ

nafsun	fauqa	hamdun	kamsun	därun	waznun
spirit	*top*	*praise*	*five*	*house*	*weight*

لُ طْ فُ   كِ ذْ بُ   خُ بْ زُ   عِ لْ مُ   زَ هْـ رُ   جِ سْ رُ

lutfun	kidbun	kubzun	ilmun	zahrun	jisrun
kindness	*lie*	*bread*	*knowledge*	*flower*	*bridge*

Words of two syllables are accented on the first syllable. Three syllable words are accented on the first unless the middle syllable is closed.

DOUBLED CONSONANT التَّشْدِيدُ

When a consonant occurs twice, one after the other, without a vowel sound in between, it is written once (unlike in English) and the sign ّ called شَدَّ "shadda" is placed over it as in رَبُّ "rabbun" *Lord*.

The consonant on which ﹽ Shadda is placed has to be distinctly pronounced twice. e.g.

فُ كِّ رَ   دُ بُّ   قَ صَّ   مَ دَّ   ظَ نَّ   شَ دَّ   شَ مَّ

fukkira   dubbun qassa madda   zanna   shadda shamma

thought over   bear   to cut to stretch to assume to harden to smell

A consonant is doubled, and receives Shadda, only when a vowel
precedes and follows it. The vowel sign is placed over this diacritic sign in
case of "fatha" or "damma" but underneath, if the vowel is "kasra" e.g.:

ﹽَ   ﹽُ   ﹽِ

All consonants admit of being doubled and take the Shadda which is
also known as "Tashdid".

CHANGING SHAPES OF THE ALPHABET

Those who study Arabic language for the first time, meet with the problem of recognising Arabic letters when they combine to form words. A student who has mastered the English alphabet can recognise the letters in a word, because the shape of English letters (Roman script) is constant whether they stand alone or form part of a word. But such is not the case with Arabic characters. In manuscript or in print, letters are interwoven with one another and form what may be called ligatures. A letter is written in slightly different form in a word according to whether it;

1. stands alone,   e.g. دع

2. constitutes the initial letter,   عاد

3. is joined to a preceding and a following letter,   فعل

4. constitutes the final letter in a word.   سمع

Note the shape of letter ع in the second, the third and fourth example where it occurs in the beginning, middle and the final positions respectively.

The following chart illustrates the above variations :—

	Examples		(3) Terminal letter	(2) Joined to the preceding and following letters	(1) Initial letter	Alone
(3)	(2)	(1)				
ماء	باز	أبٌ	با	بأ	أ	أ
mäa	*baaz*	*ab*				
water	*hawk*	*father*				
قَلْبُ	كَبِيرٌ	بَيْثٌ	ـب	ـبـ	بـ	ب
qalb	*kabir*	*bait*				
heart	*big*	*house*				

Examples			(3) Terminal letter	(2) Joined to the preceding and following letters	(1) Initial letter	Alone
(3)	(2)	(1)				
بِنْتُ	كِتَابُ	تِيْنُ	ـت	ـتـ	تـ	ت
bint girl	kitäb book	tin fig				
حَدِيْثُ	كَثِيْرُ	ثَمَرُ	ـث	ـثـ	ثـ	ث
hadit talk	katir abundant	tamar fruit				
مُزْعِجُ	شُجَاعُ	جِسْرُ	ـج	ـجـ	جـ	ج
muzaij annoying	shujäa brave	jisr bridge				
مِلْحُ	بَحْرُ	حِبْرُ	ـح	ـحـ	حـ	ح
milh salt	bahr sea	hibr ink				
شَيْخُ	نَخْلُ	خُبْزُ	ـخ	ـخـ	خـ	خ
shaik old man	nakl date-palm	kubz bread				
جَدِيْدُ	مَدْرَسَةُ	دَرْسُ	ـد	ـد	د	د
jadid new	madrasa school	dars lesson				
مُنْذُ	مَذْهَبُ	ذَرَّةُ	ـذ	ـذ	ذ	ذ
mundu since	madhab faith	darra atom				
وَزِيْرُ	مِرْوَحَةُ	رَأْسُ	ـر	ـر	ر	ر
wazer minister	mirwaha fan	räs head				
رَمْزُ	مِيْزَانُ	زَمِيْلُ	ـز	ـز	ز	ز
ramz sign/symbol	mezän scales	zamel colleague				

Examples			(3) Terminal letter	(2) Joined to the preceding and following letters	(1) Initial letter	Alone
(3)	(2)	(1)				
مَجلِسٌ majlis assembly	مِسْمارٌ mismär nail	سَماء samäa sky	س	ـسـ	ـس	س
حَشِيشٌ hashish grass	كَشّافٌ kashshäf scout	شَمسٌ shams sun	ش	ـشـ	ـش	ش
قَفَصٌ qafas cage	مِصباحٌ misbah lamp	صَيفٌ saif summer	ص	ـصـ	ـص	ص
مَرِيضٌ mared sick	فَضْلٌ fadl favour	ضامِنٌ dämin guarantor	ض	ـضـ	ـض	ض
غَلَط galat mistake	مَطار matär airport	طِفْلٌ tifl child	ط	ط	ط	ط
حَفِظَ hafeza to keep	مَنْظَر manzar sight	ظَرفٌ zarf envelope	ظ	ظ	ظ	ظ
بَيْعٌ baia selling	طَعام taäm food	عِنَب inab grape	ح	ـعـ	ـع	ع
بَلِيغٌ baleg eloquent	بَبْغاء babgäu parrot	غُلامٌ guläm boy	خ	ـغـ	ـغ	غ
شَرِيف shareef noble	نَفْع nafa gain	فَرد fard individual	ـف	ـفـ	ـفـ	ف

Examples			(3) Terminal letter	(2) Joined to the preceding and following letters	(1) Initial letter	Alone
(3)	(2)	(1)				
أُفُق ufaq horizon	بَقَرة baqara cow	قَلَم qalam pen	ـق	ـقـ	قـ	ق
سَمَك samak fish	مَرْكَب markab ship	كَشْكَوْل kashkawl note-book	ـك	ـكـ	كـ	ك
قُفْل qufl lock	جِلْد jild skin	لَحْم lahm mutton	ـل	ـلـ	لـ	ل
شَكْل shakl figure	مُتَكَلِّم mutakallim speaker	كُلِّية kulliya college	كل	ـكلـ	كلـ	كل
كَرِيمٌ karim generous	نَمِر namir tiger	مَطَر matar rain	م	ـمـ	مـ	م
وَطَن watan country	مِنْقار minqär beak	نَهْر nahr river	ـن	ـنـ	نـ	ن
وَجْهُ wajh face	مُهاجِر muhäjir emigrant	هِلال hiläl crescent	ـه	ـهـ	هـ	هـ
حَوٌّ jaww atmosphere	قَوْمِ qaum people	وَهْمُ wahm suspicion	ـو	ـو	و	و
كُرْسِيٌّ kursi chair	حَيَوان haiwän animal	يَد yad hand	ـى	ـيـ	يـ	ى

Broadly speaking, the shape of a letter does not undergo a radical change when in the last position.

e.g.   1. ع in بيع   2. ل in قفل   3. ح in ملح   4. ت in بنت

But while in the middle position i.e. preceded and followed by other letters, only the initial portion of the letter is used,

e.g.   ع "ـعـ"   ط "ـطـ"   ص "ـصـ"   س "ـسـ"

ج "ـجـ"   هـ "ـهـ"   م "ـمـ"   ل "ـلـ"

ك "ـكـ"   ق "ـقـ"   ف "ـفـ"   ت "ـتـ"

Minute semi-circles are used when ب ، ت ، ث ، س ، ش ، ن ، ى ، are used in the middle; بينتك bayyantuka *I made clear to you* when splitted would show that it consists of these letters ب ى ن ت ك

These six letters ا ، د ، ذ ، ر ، ز ، و cannot be joined to the letters that follow.

Illustrations : [See Chart] اب ـ درس ـ مذهب ـ راس ـ زميل ـ وهم

Note : Nouns and adjectives, when indefinite and in the singular number, should be read with double ٌ "un" (nunation) at the end. For example the first word in the above chart اب *father* should be read as "abun", likewise other nouns and adjectives.

DEFINITE ARTICLE الشمسية والقمرية " ال "
THE SUN LETTERS AND THE MOON LETTERS

ال is the definite article of Arabic language, it is the equivalent of the word "The" in English.

Any noun or adjective without ال is considered indefinite. There is no particular sign for the indefinite as "a" in English.

Nouns and Adjectives, when indefinite and in the singular number, end with double vowel marks e.g.

بيتٌ   جميلةٌ   كِتَابٌ

house   *beautiful*   *book*

But when these words are made definite by adding ال they will end with a single vowel mark only, e.g.

البيتُ *the house,* الجميلةُ *the beautiful,* الكتـابُ *the book*

Note: The definite article ال is prefixed to the nouns and adjectives it defines. It does not stand alone. Compare the following words with and without ال

البيتُ : بيتٌ   الجميلةُ : جميلةٌ   الكتـابُ : كتابٌ

The letters of the alphabet are divided into Sun letters الحروف الشمسية "alhuruf ushshamsiya" and the Moon letters الحروف القمريـة "al hurufu al qamariya."

The Sun letters are the dentals ت ث د ذ ر ز س ش ص ض ط ظ ل ن They are called so because the first letter of the word شمس *Sun* is ش which belongs to this category. When the definite article ال is prefixed to a noun or an adjective beginning with any one of the Sun letters, the ل, being a sun letters itself, is assimilated i.e. ل is not pronounced, thought it is written.

e.g. الشَّمس	الرَّجل	النَّصيحة	الدِّين	السَّنة
as - shams	ar - rajul	an - naseeha	ad - deen	as - sana
the sun	*the man*	*the advice*	*the religion*	*the year*

In the above words the ل of the definite article is not pronounced, and the letter next to it is pronounced twice, and "shadda" ّ is written over the initial Sun letter.

The Moon letters are: ا ب ج ح خ ع غ ف ق ك م و ه ى They are so called because the word قمر *moon*, begins with one of these letters. In case the definite article ال is prefixed to any word whose initial letter belongs to this category, ل is both written and pronounced:

القمر	الحمد	الفاكهة
al - qamar	al-hamd	al-fäkiha
the moon	*the praise*	*the fruit*

Some Arab Grammarians instead of dividing the letters into Sun letters and Moon letters, classify the definite article as ال الشمسية and ال القمرية The Sun al and the Moon al.

THE WEAK LETTERS حروف العلة

Three of the consonants ا و ى are named as حروف العلة al-huruf al-illa i.e. "weak" or "irregular" letters. These three letters are often interchanged or dropped under the influence of other letters e.g. قول becomes قال Consonants other than ا و ى are known as الحروف الصحيحة the "Sound letters" because under no circumstances they are dropped.

THE SHORTENED ALIF الالف المقصورة

There are some words where ا is indicated not in its full shape but by a short vertical stroke. This is known as الالف المقصورة the "shortened alif." However this does not change the pronunciation.

e.g. سعى، ارتضى، المصطفى، المرتضى، موسى، عيسى.

The letter ى with which these words end is not pronounced.

THE STRETCHED ALIF الالف الممدودة

In a word, when Hamza comes immediately after a vowelless الف the sign آ called "madda" «مـدّ» *stretched* is written on الف. This "alif" is lengthened while pronouncing the word. This is called الالف الممدودة the "stretched" or "extented" alif.

e.g. حمرآء   سودآء   بيضـآء
red   black   white

THE NUMERALS

The numerals used in many parts of the world are known as Arabic numerals, though they are slightly different from those used by the Arabs.

The numerals are :-

١ ٢ ٣ ٤ ٥ ٦ ٧ ٨ ٩ ٠
1 2 3 4 5 6 7 8 9 0

In manuscript, number two is usually written as < The zero is indicated by a point " "

Arabic is both written and read from the right to the left, but the numerals are written and read as in English, examples are given below:

١٩٧٦   ١٩٧٠   ١٩٥٦   ١٢٠٤   ١٨٢٥
1976   1970   1956   1204   1825

LESSON FIVE

PARTS OF SPEECH — اجزاء الكلام (الجملة)

CLASS ROOM — حجرة الدراسة

1. The class room is a place in which the students gather before the teachers, who explain the lessons and write notes on the blackboard with the chalkpiece.

(١) حُجرَةُ الدِّرَاسَةِ هِيَ الْمَكانُ الَّذى يَجْتَمِعُ فِيهِ الطُّلابُ أمامَ الاساتِذَةِ الَّذينَ يَشْرَحُونَ الدُّرُوسَ وَيَكْتُبُونَ التَّطْبِيقات عَلَى السَّبُّورَةِ بِالطَّبَاشِيرِ .

2. Every student sits on the chair and in front of him is the table. The book, the pen and note-books are on it.

(٢) وَكُلُّ طَالِبٍ يَجْلِسُ عَلَى الْكُرْسِيّ وَ أمامَهُ مِنْضَدَةٌ عَلَيْهَا الْكِتَاب وَالْقَلَمُ وَالْكَشَاكِيلُ .

3. On the wall there is the map of India, on which are (shown) the location of cities in India and the locations of industry and agriculture. These are in red, white green, yellow, blue, black and brown colours.

(٣) وَعَلَى الْحَائِطِ خَرِيطَةُ الْهِنْدِ وَبِها مِنْ مَوَاقِعِ الْمُدُنِ بِالْهِنْدِ وَ مَوَاقِعِ الصِّنَاعَةِ وَالزِّرَاعَةِ وَبِها مِنَ الألْوانِ الاحْمَرِ والابْيَضِ وَالاخْضَرِ والازْرَقِ وَالآسْوَدِ والْبُنّى .

4. It is a place where a black-board is found. It is (used) for explaining the lessons, writing the questions, answers and exercises for (concerning) all subjects.

(٤) وَ هِيَ الْمَكَانُ الَّذِى يُوجَدُ فِيهِ سَبُّورَةٌ سَوْدَاءَ لِشَرْحِ الدُّرُوس وَكِتَابَةِ الاسْئِلَةِ وَالاجْوِبَة وَالتَّمْرِيناتِ لِسائِرِ المَواد .

5. It is a place in which the teacher asks the students questions concerning the previous lessons. Then he explains (to them) the present lessson. In this manner the teacher knows the capacity of the students for understanding and memorising the lessons.

(٥) وَ هِيَ الْمَكَانُ الَّذِى يَسْأَلُ فِيهِ المُدَرِّسُ الطُّلابَ فِى الدُّرُوس السَّابِقَةِ ثُمَّ يَقُومُ المُدَرِّسُ وَيَشْرَحُ الدَّرْسَ الحَاضِرَ وَبِذَلِكَ يَعْرِفُ مَدَى قُدْرَةِ الطُّلابِ مِنَ الْفَهْم وَاسْتِذْكارِ الدُّرُوس .

The above sentences are formed by a group of words. A sentence. which conveys complete sense is called الجملة المفيدة The parts of speech or sentence are called اجزاء الجملة

Arab Grammarians have divided the parts of speech into three categories : (1) إسم Noun, (2) فعل Verb, (3) حرف Particle. But it is such a broad division that Adjectives, Pronouns, Demonstrative Pronouns are catalogued as اسماء Nouns. Prepositions, Interjections and Conjunctions are classified as حروف Particles, افعال the Verbs are almost the same as in English.

In sentence No. 1 حجرة الدراسة *class room,* هى *it,* مكان *place,*
الذى *which,* الطلاب *the students,* الاساتذة *the teachers* are grouped
under اسماء *Nouns.* In the same sentence يجتمع *gather,* is فعل
Verb and فى *in,* is حرف *Particle*

Each part of speech and its different classifications will be dealt with
separately

VOCABULARY

häit *wall*	حائط ـ حيطان	tälib *student*	طالب ـ طلاب
karita *map*	خريطة	akdar *green*	اخضر
alhind *India*	الهند	asfar *yellow*	اصفر
Laun *colour*	لون ـ الوان	azraq *blue*	ازرق
samia *to hear*	سمع ـ يسمع	aswad *black*	اسود
sämia *hearer*	سامع	ala *on*	على : فوق
abyad *white*	ابيض	fi *in*	فى
hujra *room*	حجرة ـ حجرات	rakiba *to ride*	ركب ـ يركب
hujra-t-al diräsa *class room*	حجرة الدراسة	räkib *rider*	راكب
hiya *she / it*	هى	darräja *bicycle*	دراجة ـ دراجات
makan *place*	مكان ـ امكنة	fataha *to open*	فتح ـ يفتح
ijtamaa *to gather*	اجتمع ـ يجتمع	miftah *key*	مفتاح
ahmar *red*	احمر	bäb *door*	باب ـ ابواب

zaraa *to cultivate*	زرع - يزرع	qalam *pen*	قلم - اقلام
falläh *peasant*	فلاح - فلاحون	qasab assukkar *sugar cane*	قصب السكر
kareem *generous*	كريم	täus *peacock*	طاؤوس
watan *country*	وطن	shajar *tree*	شجر - اشجار
azim *great*	عظيم	matar *rain*	مطر
ustäd *teacher*	استاذ - اساتذة	samaa *sky*	سماء - سماوات
sharaha *to explain*	شرح - يشرح	bint *girl / daughter*	بنت - بنات
dars *lesson*	درس - دروس	dahaba *to go*	ذهب - يذهب
kataba *to write*	كتب - يكتب	dähib *one who goes*	ذاهب
kätib *writer*	كاتب	sanaa *to manufacture*	صنع - يصنع
sabbüra *blackboard*	سبورة	säni *manufacturer*	صانع
tabäshir *chalk*	طباشير	jameel *beautiful*	جميل
kull *all*	كل	arabi *arab*	عربى
jalasa *to sit*	جلس - يجلس	nazala *to descend*	نزل - ينزل
jälis *one who sits*	جالس	min *from*	من
kursi *chair*	كرسى - كراسى	jamaa *to collect*	جمع - يجمع
mindada *table*	منضدة	zahr *flower*	زهر - ازهار
kitäb *book*	كتاب - كتب	madrasa *school*	مدرسة - مدارس

ila	الى	istidkär	استذكار
towards, to		memorising	
hidä	حذاء ـ احذية	dakara	ذكر ـ يذكر
shoe		to remember	
jild	جلد	tatbeeqät	تطبيقات
leather		notes	
shab	شعب	karräsa	كراسة
people		note book	
mauqia	موقع ـ مواقع	kashkül	كشكول
location		note book	
sinaa	صناعة	bunni	بُنِّى
industry		brown	
ziräa	زراعة	kitaba	كتابة
agriculture		writing	
suäl	سوال ـ اسئلة	säir	سائر
question		all	
jawäb	جواب ـ اجوبة	mädda	مادّة ـ موادّ
answer		subject	
tamreen	تمرين ـ تمارين	säbiqa	سابقة
exercise		previous	
madä	مدى	hädira	حاضرة
range		present	
qudra	قدرة	arafa	عرف ـ يعرف
power, capacity		to know	
fahima	فهم	maidan	ميدان
to understand		ground	

The following Arabic sentences further exemplify the grammatical principle that forms the subject matter of this lesson.

TRANSLATION	MODEL SENTENCES
1. The Arabs are generous.	١. الشعب العربى كريم
2. Rain descends from the sky.	٢. ينزل المطر من السماء
3. Mahmood rode (on) the bicycle.	٣. ركب محمود الدراجة
4. The green colour is beutiful.	٤. اللون الاخضر جميل.

5. The peasant cultivates
　　sugar - cane.

٥ . يزرع الفلاح قصب السكر

6. The peacock is on the tree.

٦ . الطاؤوس فوق الشجرة .

7. India is a great nation.

٧ . الهند وطن عظيم .

8. Sami went to the school.

٨ . ذهب "سامى" الى المدرسة .

9. Sita is opening the door.

٩ . تفتح "سيتا" الباب .

10. The girl is collecting the flowers.

١٠ . تجمع البنت الازهار .

11. The shoes are made of leather.

١١ . تُصنع الاحذية من الجلد .

12. Class room is open.

١٢ . حجرة الدراسة مفتوحة .

الصفة و الموصوف [النعت]

ADJECTIVE AND NOUN QUALIFIED

1. The wise man is advising.

١. الرَّجلُ الْعاقِلُ نَاصِحٌ

2. The big house is comfortable.

٢. الْبَيتُ الْكَبِيرُ مُرِيحٌ .

3. The intelligent boy is successful.

٣. الْوَلَدُ الذَّكِيُّ ناجِحٌ .

4. The red rose is fine.

٤. الْوَرْدُ الاحْمَرُ طَيِّبُ .

5. The ripe date is sweet.

٥. التَّمْرُ النَّاضِجُ حُلْوُ .

6. The two beautiful horses are loveable.

٦. الْفَرَسانِ الْجَمِيلانِ مَحْبُوْبانِ .

7. The sincere teachers are present.

٧. الْمُعَلِّمُونَ الْمُخْلِصونَ حاضِرُونَ .

8. The beautiful girl is sitting.

٨. الْبِنْتُ الْجَمِيلَةُ جَالِسَةٌ .

9. Good land is costly.

٩. الارْضُ الْجَيِّدَةُ غالِيَةٌ .

10. The clean gardens are numerous.

١٠. الْحَدَائِقُ النَّظِيفَةُ كَثِيرَةٌ .

11. The Arabic language is of high standard.

١١. اللُّغَةُ الْعَرَبِيَّةُ رَاقِيَةٌ .

12. Severe cold is painful.

١٢. الْبَرْدُ الشَّدِيدُ مُوْلِمٌ .

The adjective in Arabic is called اِسم الصفة "The noun of qualification It is one variety of a noun المركب التوصيفى or "Adjectival construction" consists of a noun qualified and the adjective. The sentences in this lesson consisit of subject and predicate. The subject itself consists of two words, the Noun qualified and the "Adjective". The first word is a noun; it is also called موصوف ـ منـعـوت *"that which is qualified"*. The second word is صفة *Adjective*, also called نعت

The adjective has to agree with the noun in respect of gender, number and definiteness, and in respect of case ending. The noun in sentence No. 1 الرجل *The man,* is masculine, singular and definite; so is its adjective العاقل *The wise.* When the same Adjective عاقل is to be used in respect of a female, it would be said الامـرأة العـاقلة ناصحـة *the wise woman is advising.*

All the twelve sentences in this lesson start with الموصوف or المنعوت *the noun qualified,* immediately followed by النعت or الصفة *adjective or description.* The above rule is followed in all but sentence No. 10. In the phrase الحدائق النظيفة *the clean gardens,* in this sentence, the adjective does not agree with the noun in respect of number الحدائق is the plural of الحديقة *The garden.* When the noun qualified is an irrational object, and is plural, masculine or feminine, its adjective would mostly be singular and in the feminine gender.

e.g. البيوت الكبيرة : *The big houses*

However when such nouns are in the dual number, their adjectives should agree with the noun.

e.g. الحُجْرتانِ الْكَبِيرتانِ مُثْقَلَتانِ : The two big rooms are locked.

الشَّجَرتانِ الْكَبِيرتانِ مُثْمِرتانِ : The two big trees are fruitful.

NOTE: In the Arabic language the noun qualified comes before the adjective

e.g. **الْوَلَدُ الذَّكِيُّ** *The intelligent boy.*

الْبِنْتُ الجَمِيلَةُ *The beautiful girl.*

VOCABULARY

aäqil	عاقل ـ عقلاء	rajul	رجل ـ رجال
wise		*man*	
näsih	ناصح	nasaha	نصح ـ ينصح
adviser		*to advise*	
bait	بيت ـ بيوت	nasiha	نصيحة ـ نصائح
house		*advice*	
murih	مريح	kabeer	كبير ـ كبار
comfortable		*big*	
daki	ذكى	walad	ولد
intelligent		*boy*	
näjih	ناجح	najaha	نجح ـ ينجح
successful		*to be successful*	
tayyib	طيب	warda	وردة
good, pleasant		*rose*	
nadaja	نضج ـ ينضج	tamar	تمر
to be ripe		*dried date*	
hulw	حلو	nädij	ناضج
sweet, charming		*ripe*	
ahabba	احب ـ يحب	faras	فرس ـ افراس
to love		*horse*	
muallim	معلم	mahbüb	محبوب
teacher		*loveable*	
muklis	مخلص	ilm	علم ـ علوم
sincere		*knowledge*	

hädir	حاضر	hadara	حضر ـ يحضر
present		to be present	
jayyd	جيد	ard	ارض ـ اراضى
excellent		earth	
hadiqa	حديقة ـ حدائق	gäliya	غالية
garden		costly	
katir	كثير	nazif	نظيف
many, much		clean	
räqiya	راقية	allugat al arabia	اللغة العربية
developed, sublime		arabic language	
shadid	شديد	bard	برد
severe		cold	
alam	ألم	mulim	مؤلم
pain		painful, distressing	
näfia	نافع	nafaa	نفع ـ ينفع
useful		to be useful	
matlüb	مطلوب	talaba	طلب ـ يطلب
desired		to seek	
mutmir	مثمرة	tamar	ثمر ـ اثمار
fruitful		fruit	
taaiba	تعب ـ يتعب	tawil	طويل
to work hard		long	
nazara	نظر ـ ينظر	mutaib	متعب
to see		tiresome, dull	
näzir	ناظر	manzar	منظر ـ مناظر
spectator, director		sight	
aarüs	عروس ـ عريس	aarüsa	عروسة
bridegroom		bride	
wafi	وفى	sadiq	صديق
faithful		friend	
akaltu	اكلت	akala	اكل ـ ياكل
I ate		to eat	

iḥdinä	اهدنا	tuffah	تفاحة
lead us		*apple*	
mustaqim	مستقيم	sirät	صراط
straight		*way*	
qitt	قط	muwä	مواء
cat		*mewing*	
yaum	يوم ـ ايام	jäaiu	جائع
day		*hungry*	
nahr	نهر	istiqläl	استقلال
river		*independence*	
qaratu	قرأتُ	järia	جارية
I read		*flowing*	
hamm	هامّ ـ مهمّ	ialän	إعلان
important		*announcement*	
rabii'	ربيع	qalansawa	قلنسوة
spring		*cap, hat*	
labisa	لبس ـ يلبس	fasl	فصل
to wear		*season, class*	
taub	ثوب ـ ثياب	maläbis	ملابس
dress		*clothes*	
shärib	شارب	shariba	شرب ـ يشرب
drinker		*to drink*	
gazir	غزير	mä	ماء ـ مياه
abundant, heavy		*water, liquid*	
katif	كثيف	sahäb	سحابَ:غيم
thick		*cloud*	
samin	سمين	tawr	ثور ـ ثيران
fat		*bull*	
härit	حارث ـ حراث	harata	حرث ـ يحرث
plough man		*to plough*	
maktaba	مكتبة	jadid	جديد
library		*new*	

hawla *around*	حول	qatafa *to pluck*	قطف ـ يقطف
mustadira *round*	مستديرة	mäida *dining-table*	مائدة
sayära *car*	سيارة ـ سيارات	hada *this*	هذا
saria' *fast*	سريع	saria *to be quick*	سرع ـ يسرع
nädir *unusual / precious*	نادر	säa' *watch*	ساعة
nasiya *to forget*	نسى ـ ينسى	ishtaraitu *I purchased*	اشتريت

The following Arabic sentences further exemplify the grammatical principle that has been explained in this lesson.

TRANSLATION	*MODEL SENTENCES*
1. Useful knowledge is desired.	١ . العلم النافع مطلوب
2. Fruit bearing tree is useful.	٢ . الشجرة المثمرة نافعة
3. The long journey is tiresome.	٣ . السفر الطويل متعب .
4. The appearance of the bride is beautiful.	٤ . منظر العروسة جميل .
5. Faithful friend is rare.	٥ . الصديق الوفى نادر .
6. I ate a sweet apple.	٦ . اكلت تفاحة حلوة .
7. Lead us to the straight path.	٧ . اهدنا الصراط المستقيم
8. A hungry cat mews.	٨ . يموء قط جائع .
9. The industrious student succeeds.	٩ . ينجح التلميذ المجتهد .
10. Independence Day is a great day.	١٠ . يوم الاستقلال يوم عظيم .

11. In India there are flowing rivers.   ١١ . فى الهند انهار جارية .

12. Spring is a beautiful season.   ١٢ . الربيع فصل جميل .

13. Wear clean dress.   ١٣ . البس ثوبا نظيفا .

14. I drank cold water.   ١٤ . شربت ماء باردا .

15. Abundant rain fell.   ١٥ . نزل مطر غزير .

16. Thick clouds are on the sky.   ١٦ . السحاب الكثيف فى السمآء .

17. The two fat bulls are ploughing.   ١٧ . الثوران السمينان يحرثان .

18. The new book is in the library.   ١٨ . الكتاب الجديد فى المكتبة .

19. I plucked a red rose.   ١٩ . قطفت وردة حمرآء .

20. We sat around a round table.   ٢٠ . جلسنا حول مائدة مستديرة .

21. This is a fast car.   ٢١ . هذه سيارة سريعة .

22. I purchased a precious watch.   ٢٢ . اشتريت ساعة نادرة .

23. This is a black cap.   ٢٣ . هذه قلنسوة سوداء .

24. I read an important announcement.   ٢٤ . قرأت اعلانا هاما .

GENDER المذكر والمؤنث

With regard to gender, Arabic nouns are divided into two categories:
(1) مذكر *masculine* and (2) مؤنث *feminine*. It is essential to know the gender of all kinds of nouns as the verbs and adjectives have to agree in respect of the gender of their subjects and the nouns qualified.

(a) Agreements of the verb with its subject:

Hamid wrote.   كَتَبَ حامد

Fatima wrote.   كَتَبَتْ فاطِمَة

Wheras for حامد the verb used is كتب, for فاطمة the verb used is كتبت; though the verb is same, in the first example it is masculine and in the second it is feminine.

(b) Agreement of the adjective with the noun qualified (See Lesson Six).

The intelligent boy.   الْوَلَدُ الذَّكِيُّ

The intelligent girl.   الْبِنْتُ الذَّكِيَّةُ

Mark the "ة" at the end of the feminine adjective.
Feminines are of two kinds.

(1) المؤنث الحقيقى *the natural or real feminines.* These are nouns denoting females.

e.g.   إمرأة   أُخْت   أُمّ
         woman   *sister*   *mother*

(2) مؤنث غير حقيقى *unreal* or "*supposed feminines.*"

e.g.   أرضٌ   شَمْسٌ   مَدِينَةٌ
         earth   *sun*   *city*

Masculine nouns do not require any sign to signify their gender. But the feminine nouns usually end in three specific ways:

(a) Feminines ending with ة "

         جميلة   نِعْمَةٌ   قُدْرَةٌ   ظُلْمَةٌ
         beautiful   *blessing*   *power*   *darkness*

خَلِيفَةٌ *caliph* and عَلامَةٌ *very learned*, are exceptions.

(b) Feminines ending with الالف المقصورة "the shortened alif"

حَشْنى	كُبْرى	بُشْرى	حَمْرى
noble lady	*big*	*good news*	*red*

(c) Feminines ending with الالف الممدودة "the stretched alif"

بَيْضآء	سَوْدآء	صَحْرآء	كِبْرِيآء
fair lady	*black*	*desert*	*pride*

Here is a list of nouns which are feminine though they are devoid of the signs to that effect.

(a) Parts of the body which are in pairs. But حاجب *eye-brow* is masculine.

اذن	فخذ	ثدى	كتف	يد	كف
ear	*thigh*	*breast*	*shoulder*	*hand*	*palm*

ساق	رجل	قدم	سن	اصبع	عين
shank	*leg*	*foot*	*tooth*	*finger*	*eye*

(b) Some natural objects which are feminine by mere usage:

نفس	أرض	نار	ريح	شمس	عين
soul	*earth*	*fire*	*wind*	*sun*	*fountain*

(c) Some objects which are occasionally used as masculine:

دار	سماء	عصا	خمر	بئر	فرش
house	*sky*	*staff*	*wine*	*well*	*bed*

كأس	جهنم	فردوس	حرب	سكين	لسان
cup	*hell*	*garden*	*war*	*knife*	*language*

The names of countries, cities and tribes are used as feminine:

هند	مدراس	قريش
India	*Madras*	*Quraish*

LESSON EIGHT

SINGULAR, DUAL AND PLURAL   ‏"المفرد والمثنى والجمع"‏

A peculiar feature of the Arabic language is that its nouns, adjectives and verbs have three numbers. In this respect it is akin to Sanskrit.

1. Singular ‏مُفرَد ـ واحِد‏

2. Dual ‏تَثنِية‏

3. Plural ‏جَمع‏

As has been mentioned earlier the adjectives of the noun qualified (lesson six) and the predicate of the subject (lesson nine) should agree with each other in respect of number. e.g.

A sincere servant came. ‏جاءَ خادِمُ مُخْلِصُ‏ Singular ‏مفرد‏

Two sincere servants came ‏جاءَ خادِمانِ مُخْلِصانِ‏ Dual ‏تثنية‏

Many sincere servants came. ‏جاءَ خُدَّامُ مُخْلِصُونَ‏ Plural ‏جمع‏

Agreement of the predicate with the subject, in respect of number :

e.g. The carpenter is working ‏النَّجَّار عامِلُ‏ Singular ‏مفرد‏

The two carpenters are working. ‏النَّجَّارانِ عامِلانِ‏ Dual ‏تثنية‏

Many carpenters are working. ‏النَّجَّارونَ عامِلونَ‏ Plural ‏جمع‏

The dual is formed by adding ‏ان‏ to the singular in the Nominative case and by ‏ين‏ in the Accusative and Genetive cases. A word in the dual number does not admit ‏التنوين‏ *Nunation*

Singualr		Dual
house	‏بَيْتُ‏	‏بَيْتَيْنِ‏ or ‏بَيْتَانِ‏
door	‏بابُ‏	‏بابَيْنِ‏ or ‏بابانِ‏
city	‏مَدِينَةُ‏	‏مَدِينَتَيْنِ‏ or ‏مَدِينَتَانِ‏

There are two kinds of plurals in Arabic, الجمع السالم *"the sound plural"* and الجمع المكسر *"the broken plural."* When a plural retains all the vowels and consonants of the singular and is based on its pattern, it is known as الجمع السالم. Whereas الجمع المكسر varies very much from its singular.

In most of the authoritative Arabic dictionaries, the plural of all categories of nouns are mentioned along with their meanings.

Some examples of الجمع السالم مذكر *The Sound Plural Masculine :*

	Plural			Singular
Writer	كاتِبِيْنَ	or	كاتِبُوْنَ	كاتِبٌ
Believer	مُؤْمِنِيْنَ	or	مُؤْمِنُوْنَ	مُؤْمِنٌ
Learned	عالِمِيْنَ	or	عالِمُوْنَ	عالِمٌ
Egyptian	مِصْرِيِّيْنَ	or	مِصْرِيُّوْنَ	مِصْرِيٌّ

Some Examples of الجمع المكسر *The broken Plural :*

	Plural	Singular		Plural	Singular
man	رجال	رَجُل	food	اطعمة	طَعام
blue	زُرَق	ازرق	youth	فتيان	فَتى
black	سُود	اشوَد	red	حُمُر	احْمَر
guest	اضْياف	ضَيْف	ass	حَمِير	حِمار
hero	ابْطال	بَطَل	earth	اراضى	ارْض
loaf	ارْغِفَة	رَغِيْف	group	فِرَق	فِرْقَة
boy	صبيان	صبى	student	طَلَبَة	طالِب
neck	اعْناق	عُنُق	book	كُتُب	كِتاب

The plural of مرأة *woman* is نساء *women*. Besides the nouns and adjectives, verbs and pronouns too are converted into dual and plural numbers.

LESSON NINE

THE NOMINAL SENTENCE   الجملة الاسمية (المبتدأ والخبر)

THE SUBJECT AND PREDICATE

1. Knowledge is light.	١ . العِلْمُ نُورُ
2. The two teachers are present.	٢ . المُعَلِّمانِ حاضِرانِ .
3. The engineers are experts.	٣ . المُهَنْدِسُونَ ماهِرونَ .
4. The students are playing.	٤ . الطُّلابُ لاعِبُونَ .
5. Fatima is intelligent.	٥ . فاطِمَةُ ذَكِيَّةُ .
6. The two girls are writing.	٦ . البِنْتانِ كاتِبَتانِ .
7. The mothers are kind.	٧ . الامَّهاتُ رَحِيماتُ .
8. The schools are open.	٨ . المَدارِسُ مَفْتُوحَةُ .

All these Arabic sentences consist of two nouns, but in the English translation, invariably the auxiliary verbs "is" and "are" are used to complete the predicate. Though the verbs are not written, all the same the very construction of the sentence presupposes the presence of the verb therein. Therefore the first word of each of the above sentences is called مبتدأ *Subject,* and the second word خبر *Predicate.*

Each of the above sentences is called الجملة الاسمية the *Nominal sentence,* because it starts with اسم *a Noun.*

1. Both the subject and the predicate in each of the above sentences are in the Nominative case مرفوع.   They end with ُ which is the sign of the nominiative.

2. Generally المبتدأ *the Subject* would be definite and الخبر *the Predicate* indefinite. Note the difference in the meaning of the following :

1. The book is new.	الْكِتَابُ جَدِيدٌ
2. The new book.	الْكِتَابُ الْجَدِيدُ
3. A new book.	كِتَابٌ جَدِيدٌ
4. This is a new book.	هذا كِتَابٌ جَدِيدٌ

3. The Predicate has to agree with its Subject in respect of number and gender.

4. When the Subject is the plural of any irrational noun the Predicate could be singular feminine (vide sentence No.8).

5. Particles belonging to groups of كان and انّ bring about certain vowel changes in respect of مبتدأ *Subject* and خبر *Predicate*. These changes are dealt with in lessons Twenty and Twenty - one.

Note : The subjects in sentences Nos. 1, 2, 3 and 4 are masculine and singular, dual and plural numbers respectively. Therefore there is agreement between the subject and the predicate.

Subjects in sentences Nos. 5, 6 and 7 are feminine and in the singular, dual and plural numbers respectively. In all these sentences the predicates are feminine and in accordance with the number of their subjects.

In sentence No.8 the subject, مدارس *schools*, (which is an irrational object) is in the plural number, therefore its predicate, مفتوحة *open* is a feminine - singular. The same rule applies to phrases which consist of موصوف *noun qualified* and صفة *adjective* (vide lesson six).

In the following table the agreement of الخبر *the predicate* with المبتدأ *the subject* in respect of gender and number is clarified further.

Feminine : مونث

مفرد ـ	Singular – The woman is good.	المَرأةُ صالِحَةٌ .
تثنية ـ	Dual – The two women are good.	المَراتانِ صالِحَتانِ .
جمع ـ	Plural – Many women are good.	النِّساءُ صالِحاتٌ .

Masculine : مذكر

مفرد ـ	Singular – The man is good.	الرَّجُلُ صالِحٌ .
تثنية ـ	Dual – The two men are good.	الرَّجُلانِ صالِحانِ .
جمع ـ	Plural – Many men are good.	الرِّجالُ صالِحُونَ .

Irrational : غير العاقل

مفرد ـ	Singular – The star is shining.	الكوكَبُ لامِعٌ .
تثنية ـ	Dual – The two stars are shining.	الكَوكَبانِ لامِعانِ .
جمع ـ	Plural – Many stars are shining.	الكَواكِبُ لامِعَةٌ .

VOCABULARY

sultän *monarch*	سلطان	nür *light*	نور
aadala *to act justly*	عدل ـ يعدل	muhandis *engineer*	مهندس
aädil *just person*	عادل	handasa *engineering*	هندسة
tijära *trade*	تجارة	laaiba *to play*	لعب ـ يلعب

tājir	تاجر	läib	لاعب
merchant		*player*	
amin	أُمين	kätib	كاتب
trustworthy		*writer*	
tibb	طب	umm	ام : والدة
medicine		*mother*	
tabib	طبيب	ab	اب : والد
physician		*father*	
mähir	ماهر	rahim	رحيم
expert		*merciful ; kind*	
shams	شمس	madrasa	مدرسة ـ مدارس
sun		*school*	
qamar	قمر	imra	امرأة ـ نساء
moon		*woman*	
daü	ضوء	sälih	صالح
light		*good*	
mudi	مضيء	salaha	صلح ـ يصلح
luminous		*to be good*	
talaa	طلع ـ يطلع	kaukab	كوكب ـ كواكب
to rise		*star*	
tälia	طالع	lämia	لامع : براق
rising ; ascending		*shining*	
tifl	طفل ـ اطفال	gurfa	غرفة
child		*room*	
näma	نام ـ ينام	gurfa at - tijära	غرفة التجارة
to sleep		*chamber of commerce*	
naum	نوم	atät	أثاث
sleep		*furniture*	
dahika	ضحك ـ يضحك	wäsia	واسع
to laugh		*spacious*	
basama	بسم ـ يبسم	jaww	جو
to smile		*atmosphere*	

bäsim *smiling*	باسم ـ مبتسم	latif *gentle*	لطيف
waqt *time*	وقت	aljins al-latheef *the fair sex*	الجنس اللطيف
laila *night*	للة	harr *heat; warmth*	حر ـ حرارة
qasura *to be short*	قصر	miqyas alharara *thermometer*	مقياس الحرارة
qasir *short*	قصير	jundi *soldier*	جندى
shujäa *courageous*	شجاع	tashjia *encouragement*	تشجيع
qadira *to be able*	قدر ـ يقدر	qädir *able*	قادر
qadir *powerful*	قدير	kataba *to lecture*	خطب ـ يخطب
darra *to harm*	ضر ـ يضر	katib *orator; lecturer*	خطيب
darar *loss*	ضرر : خسارة	waraq *paper*	ورق ـ اوراق
rabiha *to gain*	ربح ـ يربح	naaima *to be soft*	نعم ـ ينعم
ribh *profit*	ربح	niama *blessing*	نعمة
gaba *to disappear*	غاب ـ يغيب	nädir *fresh; beautiful*	ناضر
gäib *absent*	غائب	hadid *iron*	حديد
dahab *gold*	ذهب	taima *to taste*	طعم ـ يطعم
madin *metal; mine*	معدن	taäm *food*	طعام

rafaa *to raise*	رفع ـ يرفع	käli *vacant*	خال
rafia *high*	رفيع : مرتفع : عال	dawät *ink bottle*	دواة
shäria *road*	شارع ـ شوارع	mamlu *filled up*	مملوء
dayyq *narrow*	ضيق	mazaha *to joke*	مزح ـ يمزح
madina *city*	مدينة ـ مدن	matam *restaurant*	مطعم
amara *to be inhabited*	عمر	aamila *to do; act*	عمل ـ يعمل
aämir *populous, full*	عامر	aämil *doer; worker*	عامل
jahada *to endeavour*	اجتهد ـ يجتهد	jahada *to struggle*	جاهد ـ يجاهد
mujtahid *industrious*	مجتهد	qalam arrasas *pencil*	قلم الرصاص

The model sentences given below further exemplify the grammatical principle discussed in this lesson:

TRANSLATION	*MODEL SENTENCES*
1. The room is narrow.	١ . الغرفة ضيقة .
2. The furniture is new.	٢ . الاثاث جديد .
3. The earth is spacious.	٣ . الارض واسعة .
4. The water is cold.	٤ . الماء بارد .
5. The weather is pleasant.	٥ . الجو لطيف .

6. The heat is severe.	٦ . الحرارة شديدة
7. The monarch is just.	٧ . السلطان عادل .
8. The merchant is trust-worthy.	٨ . التاجر امين .
9. The physician is an expert.	٩ . الطبيب ماهر .
10. The sun is rising.	١٠ . الشمس طالعة .
11. The moon is luminous.	١١ . القمر مضيىء .
12. The stars are shining.	١٢ . الكواكب لامعة .
13. The child is sleeping.	١٣ . الطفل نائم .
14. The two boys are laughing.	١٤ . الولدان ضاحكان .
15. The girl is smiling.	١٥ . البنت باسمة .
16. Time is fleeting.	١٦ . الوقت سريع .
17. The day is long.	١٧ . اليوم طويل .
18. The night is short.	١٨ . الليلة قصيرة .
19. The soldier is brave.	١٩ . الجندى شجاع .
20. God is powerful.	٢٠ . الله قادر .
21. The apple is sweet.	٢١ . التفاحة حلوة .
22. The sermon is eloquent.	٢٢ . الخطبة بليغة .
23. The rain is abundant.	٢٣ . المطر غزير .

24. The paper is smooth.	٢٤ . الورق ناعم .
25. The flowers are fresh.	٢٥ . الازهار ناضرة .
26. Iron is useful.	٢٦ . الحديد نافع .
27. The food is ready.	٢٧ . الطعام حاضر .
28. The room is vacant.	٢٨ . الغرفة خالية .
29. The ink-pot is full.	٢٩ . الدواة مملوءة .
30. Much joking is harmful.	٣٠ . المزاح الكثير مضر .
31. The trade is profitable.	٣١ . التجارة رابحة .
32. The boys are writing.	٣٢ . الاولاد كاتبون .
33. The workers are absent.	٣٣ . العمال غائبون .
34. The lady teachers are present.	٣٤ . المعلمات حاضرات .
35. Gold is a metal.	٣٥ . الذهب معدن .
36. The sky is high.	٣٦ . السماء مرتفعة .
37. The road is narrow.	٣٧ . الشارع ضيق .
38. The city is populous.	٣٨ . المدينة عامرة .
39. The duck is fat.	٣٩ . البطة سمينة .
40. The two girls are hard-working.	٤٠ . البنتان مجتهدتان .

LESSON TEN

THE POSSESSIVE   المضاف والمضاف اليه

1. The creator of the universe is one.	١ . خالِقُ العالَمِينَ واحِدُ .
2. God's earth is spacious.	٢ . ارضُ الله واسعة .
3. The people of India are good.	٣ . اهلُ الهِندِ طَيِّبُونَ .
4. The hospitality of the Arabs is famous.	٤ . جُودُ العَرَبِ مَشْهُورُ .
5. The hands of the boy are clean.	٥ . يَدا الوَلَدِ نَظِيفَتانِ .
6. The servants of the nation are popular.	٦ . خادِمُو الوطَنِ مُحِبُّونَ .
7. The students of the secondary school are playing.	٧ . طُلابُ المَدرَسَةِ الثَّانَوِيَّةِ لاعِبُونَ .
8. Fear of God is the summit of wisdon.	٨ . مَخَافَةُ الله رَاسُ الحِكْمَةِ .
9. Al Azhar University is the centre of many sciences.	٩ . جَامِعَةُ الازْهَر مَرْكَزُ العُلُومِ المُخْتَلِفةِ .

In the English language the idea of "possession" or "ownership" is conveyed by using apostrophe and s ('s) or the preposition "of". But "possession" or "ownership" is conveyed in Arabic by اضافة *annexation* i.e. one noun follows the other in such a manner that the former governs the latter in the genitive case.

e.g. God's earth	ارضُ الله
the king's daughter	بِنْتُ المَلِكِ
a king's daughter	بنتُ مَلِك

The first word in these examples is called مضاف and the second
مضاف اليه

NOTE:— 1. Both مضاف اليه and مضاف are nouns.

2. مضاف would be indefinite and مضاف اليه would either be a proper or a common noun.

3. مضاف will not accept the defininte article ال and "nunation."

4. Due to اضافة the مضاف اليه ends in ــِ i.e. the genitive case.

5. The dual and sound plural masculine lose their final ن due to اضافة This may be noticed in the following phrases in sentence No. 5 and No. 6 where ن is dropped from يدان and خادمون

The hands of the boy	يَدا الوَلَدِ
The servants of the nation	خادِمُو الوَطَنِ

There are other forms in Arabic which convey the idea of "possession" etc. Besides the use of possessive pronouns كتابه *his book* كتابك *your book* كتابى *my book* (vide lesson No. 12) these words are generally used: ذو *possessor, owner,* صاحب *companion,* أهل *people.*

e.g. The possessor of learning	ذو العِلمِ
The companion or the man of learning	صاحبُ العِلمِ
The people of learning (learned people)	اهلُ العِلمِ

VOCABULARY

kalij Bengal *bay of bengal*	خليج البنغال	kaliq *creator*	خالق
adab *literature*	ادب	kalaqa *to create*	خلق - يخلق

muaddab *polite*	مؤدَّب	maklüq *creatures*	مخلوق
adib *literary man*	اديب	aälam *world : universe*	عالم : الدنيا
asäs *foundation*	اساس	wähid *one*	واحد
laban *milk*	لبن : حليب	Allah *God*	الله
baqara *cow*	بقرة	ahl *family, people*	اهل : اسرة
balad *country*	بلد ـ بلدان	jüd *generosity*	جود : كرم
baladia *municipality*	بلدية	ashhara *to make famous*	اشهر
garb *west*	غرب	shahir *famous*	شهير : مشهور
sharq *east*	شرق : مشرق	yad *hand*	يد
shimäl *north*	شمال	istaqdama *to employ*	استخدم
junüb *south*	جنوب	kädim *servant*	خادم ـ خدام
kidma *service*	خدمة	tänawia *secondary school*	مدرسة ثانوية
qadama *to advance*	قدم	ibtidaia *elementary school*	مدرسة ابتدائية
mutaqaddim *advanced*	متقدم	kauf *fear*	خوف : مخافة
wazir *minister*	وزير ـ وزرآء	käfa *to fear*	خاف ـ يخاف
wizära *ministry*	وزارة	rais *chief, president*	رئيس
bustan *garden*	بستان : حديقة	hikma *wisdom*	حكمة

tilmid *student*	تلميذ : طالب	hakim *wise*	حكيم : عاقل
asad *lion*	اسد	kullia *college*	كلية
malik *king*	ملك ـ ملوك	jamia *university*	جامعة
mamlaka *kingdom*	مملكة	risha *feather*	ريشة ـ ريش
gäba *jungle*	غابة	kurtüm *trunk*	خرطوم
ahräm *pyramids*	اهرام	feel *elephant*	فيل
atiq *old*	عتيق : قديم	misr *Egypt*	مصر
ayn *eye*	عين : عيون	wajaba *to be necessary*	وجب ـ يجب
ajal *haste*	عجل	wäjib *essential*	واجب
ajala *wheel*	عجلة	gusn *branch*	غصن ـ اغصان
kasara *to break*	كسر ـ يكسر	fara *branch, section*	فرع ـ فروع
maksür *broken*	مكسور	farada *to suppose, to impose*	فرض
ikram *respect ; honour*	اكرام	farida *duty*	فريضة
däim *permanent*	دائم	mathaf *museum*	متحف ـ متحفة
muwaqqat *temporary*	موقّت	daif *guest*	ضيف
insän *man*	انسان	mudif *host*	مضيف

insänia *humanity*	انسانية	mudifa *hostess*	مضيفة
mushrif *superintendent*	مشرف	shareef *noble*	شريف
musäfir *traveller*	مسافر	säfara *to go on a journey*	سافر ـ يسافر
sifära *embassy*	سفارة	safir *ambassador*	سفير
räs *head ; summit*	رأس	sharrafa *to honour*	شرَّف ـ يشرِّف

The following sentences further exemplify the grammatical principles discussed in this lesson:

TRANSLATION	*MODEL SENTENCES*
1. The colour of the sky is blue.	١ . لون السماء ازرق .
2. The feather of the peacock is excellent.	٢ . ريش الطاؤوس جيد .
3. The trunk of the elephant is long.	٣ . خرطوم الفيل طويل .
4. Bay of Bengal is beautiful.	٤ . خليج بنغال جميل .
5. Character is the foundation of success.	٥ . الادب اساس النجاح .
6. The milk of the cow is sweet.	٦ . لبن البقرة حلو .
7. The Western countries are advanced.	٧ . بلدان الغرب متقدمة .
8. The Rector of Al-Azhar University visited Arabic Department of New College, Madras in 1975.	٨ . مدير جامعة الازهر قد زار قسم اللغة العربية فى الكلية الجديدة بمدراس فى سنة ١٩٧٥

9. The doors of the museum are open.   ٩ . ابواب المتحف مفتوحة .

10. The students of the Madras University.   ١٠ . تلاميذ جامعة مدراس اذكياء
    are intelligent.

11. The lion is the king of the jungle.   ١١ . الاسد ملك الغابة .

12. The pyramids of Egypt are ancient.   ١٢ . اهرام مصر عتيقة .

13. The (two) eyes of the cat are bright.   ١٣ . عينا القط لامعتان .

14. The (two) wheels of the bicycle are.   ١٤ . عجلتا الدراجة مكسورتان
    broken

15. Respect of the guests is obligatory.   ١٥ . اكرام الضيوف واجب .

16. The branch of the tree is green.   ١٦ . غصن الشجرة اخضر .

17. Acquiring knowledge is obligatory.   ١٧ . طلب العلم فريضة .

18. The teachers of the school are   ١٨ . معلمو المدرسة مسافرون .
    travelling.

19. God's mercy is permanent.   ١٩ . رحمة اللّه دائمة .

20. Man is the noblest of creation.   ٢٠ . الانسان اشرف المخلوقات .

LESSON ELEVEN

THE PRONOUN   الضمير ـ الضمائر المنفصلة

MY COUNTRY   وطنى

١ . الهِنْدُ وَطَنِى ـ هِىَ قُطْرُ غَنِىٌّ .

1. India is my country. It is a rich region.

٢ . ارضُها خِصبةٌ وصالِحَةٌ للزِّراعة وأثمارُها كَثيرةٌ وَجَوُّهَا مُعْتَدِلٌ وَسَماءها صافِيَةٌ وَخَيْراتها كَثيرةٌ

2. Her land is fertile and good for agriculture, her fruits are many. Her climate is moderate, her sky is clear and her resources are abundant.

٣ . انْهارُها كَثيرةٌ تَروى الاْنسانَ والحَيوانَ و تُسقى الزَّرعَ

3. Its rivers are many which provide water to human beings and animals. And they irrigate (agriculture) farming.

٤ . الهِندُ بَلَدُ الصِّناعَة تُكْثَرُ فيها الصِّناعاتُ المُخْتَلِفةُ وتُعتبرُ من اهَمّ مَراكِزِ الصِناعة فى آسِيا .

4. India is an industrial country. Different industries are (found) in it in abundance. It is considered to be one of the important industrial contres in Asia.

٥ . شعبُها كَريمٌ يُحِبُّ الضَّيْفَ ويُكْرِمُ الفُقَراءَ .

5. Its people are noble. They love (like) the guest and treat the poor generously.

٦ . وَطَنُنا اعظمُ جُمهُوريةٍ فِى العالَمِ .

6. Our country is the biggest democracy in the world.

7. And our army is among the strongest armies of the world.

٧. وَجَيْشُنا مِن أَقْوَى جُيُوشِ الْعَالمِ.

8. I am a soldier, a servant of my country.

٨. أنا جُنْدِئٌ خادِمٌ لِوَطَنِى.

9. This is the flag of my country, it is oblong in shape, its colours are three, and in the middle is the Ashoka wheel.

٩. هذا عَلَمُ بَلَدِى، شَكْلُهُ مُسْتَطِيلُ وأَلْوَانُهُ ثَلاثَةٌ وفِى الْوَسطِ عَجْلَةُ أُشوكا

10. India is a member of the United Nations Organisation and she plays an important role in all its activities. Our Government is endeavouring to eradicate illiteracy and to expand facilities for training and education.

١٠. والهند عضوُ فى هَيْئةِ الامم المتحدَةِ وهى تَلْعَبُ دَوْراً هاماً فى جَمِيع نشاطاتها ـ وحُكُومتنا تَبْذُلُ جُهودا للقضاء على الامية ولتوسيع المجالات للتربية والتعليم.

11. Our leaders are making efforts for the welfare of the people, for strengthening friendly relations between people (of different nations) and for world peace.

١١. كما يحاول زعماؤنا لأجل مَصْلَحة الشَّعب ولتوثيق العلاقات الوُدّية بَين الشعوب والأمن العالمى.

Pronouns are of two varieties (1) الضمائر المنفصلة "Independent pronouns" and (2) الضمائر المتصلة "Attached pronouns." The first variety of pronouns stand alone e.g. هو *he,* أَنت *you* أَنا *I.* The second variety of pronouns are suffixed :

1. to nouns : *his book*   كِتابُهُ

2. to verbs : *I wrote it*   كَتَبتُهُ

3. to prepositions : *for him*   لَهُ

In the first sentence the word وطنى *my country,* is a combination of a noun وطن *country* and a pronominal suffix ى *my.* This is الضمير المتصل *the pronoun that is attached.* These suffixes which are attached to a noun, correspond to "Possessive Pronouns" of the English language, e.g. قلمه *his pen.* When they are suffixed to prepositions and verbs they correspond to Personal Pronouns in the Objective Case.

In the first sentence itself هى *she/it* is also a pronoun. It is called الضمير المنفصل *the pronoun which is independent* or which stands alone.

In the ninth sentence هذا علم الهند *this is the flag of India,* a demonstrative pronoun has been used i.e. هذا *this.* Demonstrative Pronouns, as in English, are separate for near objects and distant objects. But, in Arabic the demonstrative pronouns أسماء الاشارة , should agree with the gender and number of the person or object intended.

List of الضمائر المنفصلة (Personal pronouns)

3rd Person Masculine :   *Examples :*

1. Singular he / it	هُوَ	He is a man	هُوَ رَجُلٌ
2. Dual they (two)	هُما	They (two) are men	هُما رَجُلانِ
3. Plural they	هُمْ	They are men	هُمْ رِجالٌ

3rd Person Feminine :

4. Singular she	هِىَ	She is a woman	هِىَ إمرَأةٌ
5. Dual they (two)	هُما	They (two) are women	هُما إمرَأتانِ
6. Plural they	هُنَّ	they are women	هُنَّ نِسْوَةٌ

2nd Person Masculine:

7. Singular: you	اَنْتَ	You are a boy.	اَنْتَ وَلَدُ
8. Dual you (two)	اَنتُما	You (two) are boys.	اَنتُما وَلَدَانِ
9. Plural You (all)	اَنتُمْ	You are boys.	اَنتُمْ اولادُ

2nd Person Feminine:

10. Singular You	اَنتِ	You are a girl.	اَنتِ بِنْتُ
11. Dual you (two)	اَنتُما	You (two) are girls.	اَنتُما بِنتانِ
12. Plural you (all)	اَنتُنَّ	You are girls.	اَنتُنّ بَناتُ

1st Person Masculine / Feminine:

13. Singular I (M & F)	اَنا	I am a boy.	اَنا وَلَدُ
		I am a girl.	اَنا بِنْتُ
14. Plural We (M & F)	نَحْنُ	We are boys.	نَحْنُ اولادُ
		We are girls.	نَحْنُ بَناتُ

VOCABULARY

as - sayid	السيد	sabaqa	سبق
Mr.		*to precede, outstrip*	
as - sayida	السيدة	säbiq	سابق : متقدم
Mrs.		*winner, ahead*	
qutr	قطر	nashita	نشط
region		*to be lively*	
gani	غنى	nashit	نشيط
rich		*energetic / active*	
änisa	آنسة : فتات	nashät	نشاط
Miss		*activity, briskness*	
saläm	سلام	kaima	خيمة
peace		*tent*	

askar *army*	عسكر	jamhūr *multitude, people*	جمهور
muaskar *army camp*	معسكر	jaish *troops*	جيش ــ جيوش
sahifa *newspaper*	صحيفة : اخبار	qawi *strong*	قوى ــ اقوى
zaaim *leader*	زعيم : رئيس	sahäfi *journalist*	صحافى
zaäma *leadership*	زعامة : رئاسة	alam *flag*	علم : راية
dafaa *to repel*	دفع ــ يدفع	shakl *figure*	شكل : صورة
difaa *defence*	دفاع	mustatil *oblong*	مستطيل
kashafa *to uncover*	كشف ــ يكشف	däira *circle*	دائرة
faqir *poor*	فقير ــ فقراَء	käshif *discoverer*	كاشف
kasib *fertile*	خصب	al-kashshafa *the scout*	الكشافة
ziräa *agriculture*	زراعة	sannafa *to compose*	صنف
mua'tadil *moderate*	معتدل	musannif *writer*	مصنف
safw *clear, pure*	صفو	shäir *poet*	شاعر
kaira *good things*	خيرة : خيرات	shair *poetry*	شعر
aazam *greatest*	اعظم	tamtilia *drama*	تمثيلية
jumhuriya *republic*	جمهورية	ukt *sister*	اخت

sabil	سبيل	qarra	قارة
way		*continent*	
murabbaa	مربع	äsia	آسيا
square		*asia*	
mutallat	مثلث	badala	بذل ـ يبذل
triangle / threefold		*to make (effort)*	
wast	وسط	juhd	جهد ـ جهود
middle		*effort*	
ashoka	اشوكا	badl-al-juhud	بذل الجهود
Ashoka (King of India)		*to make efforts*	
sayd	سيّد ـ سادة	rawwaya	روّى
master		*supply water*	
sayda	سيدة ـ سيدات	insän	انسان
mistress		*human being*	
natr	نثر	hayawan	حيَوان
prose		*animal*	
ak	اخ ـ اخوة	maut	موت
brother		*death*	
aish	عيش : حياة	habba	حبّ ـ يحب
life		*to love, like*	
sadaqa	صداقة	daif	ضيف ـ ضيوف
friendship		*guest*	
sadiq	صديق	amn	امن
friend		*peace*	
sinäaa	صناعة	al-amn-al-alami	الامن العالمى
industry		*world peace*	
qala	قلعة	maslaha	مصلحة
fort, stronghold		*interest, good*	

Note the use of pronouns in the following sentences:

TRANSLATION	MODEL SENTENCES
1. This is a rich peasant.	١ . هذا فلاح غنى .
2. This is a beautiful flower.	٢ . هذه زهرة جميلة .
3. These are two beautiful roses.	٣ . هاتان وردتان جميلتان .
4. These are expert engineers.	٤ . هؤلاء مهندسون ماهرون .
5. These are female workers in the spinning factory.	٥ . هؤلاء عاملات فى مصنع النسيج .
6. This is a book, in which there is no doubt.	٦ . ذلك الكتاب لا ريب فيه .
7. That is a heavy tank.	٧ . تلك دبابة ضخمة .
8. Those are two useful books.	٨ . ذنك كتابان نافعان .
9. Those are accountants of the company.	٩ . أولئك محاسبو الشركة .
10. She is an air hostess.	١٠ . هى مضيفة الطائرة .
11. He is a post-man.	١١ . هو ساعى البريد .
12. They two are honest police-men.	١٢ . هما شرطيان أمينان .
13. They are the brave soldiers of India.	١٣ . هم جنود الهند الشجعان .
14. They are nurses (f).	١٤ . هن ممرضات .
15. The boy who succeeds in the examination is industrious.	١٥ . الولد الذى ينجح فى الامتحان مجتهد .
16. These are (the two) guests who called on us yesterday.	١٦ . هذان الضيفان اللذان زارا بيتنا بالأمس .

LESSON TWELVE

POSSESSIVE, DEMONSTRATIVE AND RELATIVE PRONOUNS

الضمائر المنفصلة وأسماء الاشارة وأسماء الموصولة

THE CITY OF MADRAS

مَدِينَةُ مَدراس

1. Madras is a big city. Its inhabitants exceed three million persons. It is the capital of the state of Tamil Nadu. It is situated in South on the Bay of Bengal.

١. مَدِينَةُ مَدراس مَدِينَةٌ كَبِيرَةٌ. يَزِيدُ عَدَدُ سُكَّانِها عَلى ثَلاثَةِ مَلايِينَ نَسَمَة وَهِيَ عَاصِمَةُ وِلايَةِ تامل نادُو وَتَقَعُ فِى الجَنُوبِ عَلى خَلِيجِ بَنْغال.

2. The city of Madras is distinguished (distinct from others) by its moderate climate. It is not extremely hot in summer like other cities nor (or) extremely (severely) cold during winter. The city experiences seasonal rains (seasonal rains descend on it) which provide water to the animals and plants.

٢. تَمْتاز مَدِينَة مَدراس بِطَقْسِها [جَوّ] المُعْتَدِل فَهِيَ لَيْسَت شَدِيدَة الحَرارَةِ فِى الصَّيفِ كَبَقِيَّةِ المُدُنِ ولَيْسَت شَدِيدَة البُرُودَةِ فِى الشِّتاء. وَتَسْقُطُ عَلَيهَا أَمْطَارُ مَوسَمِيَّةٌ لِتَسْقِيَ الحَيوانَ والنَّبَات.

3. And therein are many ministerial offices, colleges, institutes and schools in it.

٣ . وفِيها كَثِيرٌ مِنَ الوَزاراتِ والكُلِّياتِ والمَعَاهِدِ والمَدارِسِ .

4. It is an industrial and commercial city. The ships anchor at its port and carry its goods and bring to the traders and the industrialists what is required by them from abroad.

٤ . وهِيَ مَدِينَةٌ صِناعِيَّةٌ تِجارِيَّةٌ تَرْسُو البَواخِرُ عَلى مِينائِها فَتَحْمِلُ مِنْ خَيراتِها الكَثِيرَةِ وتَنْزِلُ إلى التُّجارِ والصُّنَّاعِ ما يَحتاجُونَ إليهِ مِنَ الخارَجِ .

5. It is a horticultural [agricultural] city. Cultivation of vegetables, fruits and coconut are found in its outskirts; even as big gardens are also found in the city.

٥ . وهِيَ أيضاً مَدِينَةٌ زَراعِيَّةٌ فَتُوجَدُ فِى ضَواحِيها زِراعَةُ الخُضروات والفواكِهِ وجَوزَةِ الهِندِ كما توجدُ فِى المدينةِ حَدائِقُ كثيرةٌ .

6. An airport, highways for cars and the railway station connect her with the (other) states of India.

٦ . ويَربُطُها بِولاياتِ الهِند الاخرَى مَطارٌ جَوِّىٌّ وطُرُقٌ للسَّيَّاراتِ ومَحطةٌ للسكك الحدِيدِيَّة .

7. There are in Madras, post, telegraph and telephone offices. And on its wide roads buses, taxies and cycles ply. And its biggest highway is Mount Road.

٧ . وفِى مَدراس مَكاتِبُ للبَرِيدِ والبَرْقِ والهاتِفِ ويَجْرِى فِى شَوَارِعِها الفَسِيْحَةِ أُتوبِيس وسيَّاراتُ الاجرةِ والدَّرَّاجات وأكْبَرُ شَوَارِعِها «مَوْنْت رُود»

Those who study Arabic, as a foreign language, are puzzled at expressions like inseparable pronouns, inseparable prepositions and conjunctions. They are inseparable, because they form part of the word, and are either prefixed or suffixed to it. When these pronouns, prepositions and conjunctions (indicated by a solitary letter or more) are joined to the words, they pose a problem to the beginner. But this problem ceases to exist as the student gets familiar with the language.

	Splitted	*Expressions*
e.g. in the name of God	ب + اسم الله	باسم الله
his pen	قلم + ه	قلمه
your book	كتاب + ك	كتابك
in it	فى + ه	فيه
book and pen	كتاب + و + قلم	كتاب و قلم
and he wrote it	ف + كتب + ه	فكتبه

The pronouns that are attached الضمائر المتصلة

Suffixed to prepositions	Suffixed to nouns	Meaning	Mere suffixes	
				3rd per. Mas غائب مذكر
له**	كتابه*	him : his	١ . هُ	
لهما	كتابهما	them : their	٢ . هُما	
لهم	كتابهم	them : their	٣ . هُم	
				3rd per. Fem. غائب مؤنث
لها	كتابها	her	٤ . هَا	
لهما	كتابهما	them : their	٥ . هُما	
لهن	كتابهن	them : their	٦ . هُنَّ	

for him :(ه + ل) له**   his book :(ه + كتاب) كتابه*

2nd per. Mas

لك	كتابك	you : your كَ .٧	مخاطب مذكر
لكما	كتابكما	you : your كُما .٨	
لكم	كتابكم	you : your كُم .٩	

2nd per. Fem.

لك	كتابك	you : your كِ .١٠	مخاطب مؤنث
لكما	كتابكما	you : your كُما .١١	
لكن	كتابكن	you : your كُنَّ .١٢	

1st per. Mas / Fem.

متكلم مذكر ومونث

لى	كتابى	me : my ى .١٣	
لنا	كتابنا	us : our نا .١٤	

These are suffixed to verbs, when a personal pronoun is the direct object of a verb.

e.g. I saw her رايتها　　　　I struck him ضَرَبتُه

DEMONSTRATIVE PRONOUNS　اسماء الاشارة

For distant objects			For near objects			
plural	dual	sing	plural	dual	sing	
اولئك	ذانك	ذلك	هؤلاء	هذان	هذا	Mas
اولئك	تانك	تلك	هؤلاء	هاتان	هذه	Fem.

---

١ هذا this　　٢ ذلك that

RELATIVE PRONOUNS الاسماء الموصولة

	plural	dual	sing	
who;whom;that;which: الذى	الذين	الذان	الذى	Mas.
who: مَنْ	اللاتى	اللتان	التى	Fem.
what; what thing: ما				

VOCABULARY

istaurada	استورد	adad	عدد
to import		*number,figure*	
wäridät	واردات	sakana	سكن ـ يسكن
imports		*to reside, to be still*	
asdara	اصدر	sukkan	ساكن ـ سكان
to export		*inhabitants*	
sädirät	صادرات	miliwn	مليون
exports		*million*	
häja	حاجة	däkil	داخل
need, want		*inside, interior*	
kärij	خارج	däkili	داخلى
outside, abroad		*internal*	
käriji	خارجى	rabata	ربط ـ يربط
external		*to bind, connect*	
zäda	زاد ـ يزيد	räbita	رابطة ـ روابط
to increase		*connection*	
ziyäda	زيادة	tariq	طريق ـ طرق
increase, addition		*passage, way*	
zäid	زائد	maktaba	مكتبة ـ مكاتب
excessive		*library*	

barid	بريد	rasä al markab	رسا المركب
post ; mail		*to anchor (ship)*	
säi al barid	ساعى البريد	markab	مركب : باخرة
the postman		*ship ; steamer*	
barq	برق	mina	ميناء
lightning		*port*	
barqiya	برقية : تلغراف	mahatta	محطة
telegram		*station*	
hätif	هاتف	sikkat al hadid	سكة الحديد
wireless, telephone		*railway*	
jarä	جرى ـ يجرى	matär	مطار : محطة الطيران
to run, to flow		*airport*	
fasih	فسيح	täira	طائرة
wide, spacious		*aeroplane*	
nasaja	نسج ـ ينسج	sayära	سيارة
to weave		*automobile, car*	
mansaj	منسج	raib	ريب : شك
weaving factory		*doubt*	
nasama	نسمة ـ نسم	dabbäba	دبابة
person (in census)		*tank*	
aäsima	عاصمة	dakm	ضخم
capital		*huge, big*	
wiläya	ولاية	hisäb	حساب
state		*calculation, accounting*	
mahad	معهد	ilmul hisäb	علم الحساب
institute		*arithmetic*	
masnaa	مصنع	marida	مرض ـ يمرض
factory		*to fall sick*	
mu'tadil	معتدل	marid	مريض
moderate, proportionate		*sick person*	
rasä	رسا	mumarrida	ممرضة
anchoring		*nurse*	

taftish	تفتيش : فحص	saqata	سقط ـ يسقط
investigation		*to fall down, drop*	
sayyara ujra	سيارة اجرة : تكسى	mausim	موسم
taxi		*season*	
hamala	حمل ـ يحمل	mausimia	موسمية
to carry		*seasonal*	
hammäl	حمال	fäkiha	فاكهة ـ فواكه
porter		*fruit*	
nazzala	نزل	dähiya	ضاحية ـ ضواح
to come down		*out skirts, vicinity*	
ams	أمس : البارحة	mäza (maiz)	ماز(ميز)
yesterday		*to distinguish, set aside*	
muhäsib	محاسب	mumtäz	ممتاز
accountant		*distinguished, rare*	
sharika	شركة	taqs	طقس : جو
company		*climate*	
shurti	شرطى	shadid	شديد
policeman		*severe, hard*	
imtihän	إمتحان	hadiqa	حديقة : بستان
examination		*garden*	
bard	برد ـ برودة	kadrawät	خضروات
cold-coldness		*vegetables, greens*	
harr	حر ـ حرارة	nabt	نبت ـ نبات
hot, warmth		*plants*	

Note the use of pronouns in the following sentences :

TRANSLATION	*MODEL SENTENCES*
1. This student is active.	١ . هذا الطالب نشيط
2. This is a tent of the army camp.	٢ . هذه خيمة المعسكر
3. These are two faithful friends.	٣ . هذان صديقان وفيان .
4. These are the students of the Arab Republic of Egypt.	٤ . هؤلاء تلاميذ جمهورية مصر العربية .

5. That is a journalist.

٥ . ذلك صحفى .

6. Those are two doctors.

٦ . ذَنك طبيبان .

7. Those are two wheels of the aeroplane.

٧ . ذَنك عجلتا الطيارة .

8. Those are the leaders of the nation.

٨ . أولئك زعماء القوم .

9. He is the Defence Minister.

٩ . هو وزير الدفاع .

10. She is a girl guide (Scout).

١٠ . هى كشافة .

11. They two are authors.

١١ . هما مصنفان .

12. They are poets.

١٢ . هم شعرآء .

13. They are the sisters of Raman.

١٣ . هن اخوات «رامن» .

14. India in which we live is our country.

١٤ . الهند التى نعيش فيها وطننا .

15. One who struggled for India's independence is Mahatma Gandhi.

١٥ . الذى جاهد لاستقلال الهند هو مهاتما غاندى .

16. Those who spend their money in the way of God are noble.

١٦ . الذين ينفقون اموالهم فى سبيل الله كرماء .

INTERROGATIVES   أدوات الاستفهام

CONVERSATION BETWEEN A SHEIK AND A YOUTH	مُحادَثَةٌ بَيْنَ شَيْخ وفتى
Sheik: Peace be on you.	الشيخ : السلام عليكم
Youth: Peace be on you, Welcome	الفتى : وعليكم السلام اهلا ومرحبا
1. Sh: What is your name?	١ . ش : ما إسمك ؟
Y: My name is Abu Bakr.	ف : إسمى ابو بكر .
2. Sh: What is your age?	٢ . ش : كم عُمرُكَ ؟
Y: My age is twenty years.	ف : عُمرى عِشرُونَ سَنة .
3. Sh: In which college do you study?	٣ . ش : فى ايّ كلية تَتَعَلَّمُ ؟
Y: I study in New College in Madras.	ف : أتَعَلَّم فى الكلية الجَدِيدَة بمَدراس .
4. Sh: Are you in the Arabic Department?	٤ . ش : أ أنْت فى قِسْمِ اللُّغَةِ العَرَبِية ؟
Y: Yes. I am a student in the Arabic Department.	ف : نَعَم أنا تِلْميذُ فى قِسْمِ اللُّغَة العَرَبِية .
5. Sh: Do you love this language?	٥ . ش : هَلْ تُحبُّ هذه اللُّغَةَ ؟
Y: Yes. I love it much.	ف : نَعَم أُحِبُّها جِدّاً

6. Sh: Can you speak in Arabic (language)

٦ . ش : هَلْ تَسْتَطِيعُ أَنْ تَتَحَدَّثَ بِاللُّغَةِ العَرَبِيةِ ؟

Y: Yes, I can speak (in) Arabic (language)

ف : نَعَمْ أَسْتَطِيعُ أَنْ أَتَحَدَّثَ بِاللُّغَةِ العَرَبِيةِ .

7. Sh: Why have you chosen this language?

٧ . ش : لِماذا اِخْتَرْتَ هذِهِ اللّغَةَ ؟

Y: Because it is one of the famous languages of the world.

ف : لأِنَّها مِنْ أَشْهَرِ لُغاتِ العَالَمِ .

8. Sh: Who teaches you?

٨ . ش : مَنْ يُعَلِّمُكَ ؟

Y: Dr.Nazmi Abdul Badie, the delegate of the Al-Azhar University, teaches me.

ف : يُعَلِّمُنِى دكْتُور نَظْمِى عَبْدُ البَدِيعِ ، مَبْعُوث جامِعةِ الازْهَرِ .

9. Sh: When do you go to the college?

٩ . ش : مَتَى تَذْهَبُ اِلى الكِلِّيَةِ ؟

Y: I go to the college at 9-00 a.m.

ف : اذْهَبُ اِلى الكِلية فى السَّاعةِ التَّاسِعَةِ صَباحاً .

10. Sh: How many lectures do you attend in a day.

ش : كم مُحاضَرةً تأخُذُها فى اليَومِ ؟

Y: I attend (take) six lectures.

ف : آخُذُ سِتَّ مُحاضَراتٍ

11. Sh : Where do you go in the evening after you return to the house?

١١ . ش : أَيْنَ تَذْهَبُ فى الْمَساءِ بَعْدَ رُجُوعِكَ الى الْبَيْتِ؟

Y : I go to the sea shore in the evening.

ف : أَذْهَبُ الى شاطئ الْبَحْرِ مَساءً .

12. Sh : Do you go by car or walking?

١٢ . ش : أَتَذْهَبُ راكبا فى السَّيَّارةِ أَمْ ماشيا؟

Y : I go by car some-times and walking (during) other times.

ف : أَذْهَبُ راكبا فى السَّيارةِ أَحْيانا وماشيا أَحْيانا أُخرى .

13. Sh : Have you not seen the sea before?

١٣ . ش : أَلَم تُشاهِدِ الْبَحْرَ قَبْلَ الآنَ؟

Y : Yes indeed I have seen it several times.

ف : بَلى رأَيْتُهُ مِراراً .

14. Sh : Don't you know swimming well?

١٤ . ش : أَلا تُجِيدُ السِّباحَةَ؟

Y : I am afraid of swim-ming.

ف : أَخافُ مِنَ السِّباحَةِ .

15. Sh : How are you?

١٥ . ش : كَيْفَ حالُكَ؟

Y : Well, praise be to God.

ف : بِخَيْرٍ والحمدُ لله .

Interrogative sentences are introduced by the Particles هَل or أ . أ is prefixed to the first word of the interrogative sentence. In sentences Nos. 4 and 12 أ is prefixed to a pronoun and verb respectively. In certain cases interrogative pronouns and Adverbs are also used for making interrogative sentences.

Interrogative pronouns		Adverbs which are widely used as Interrogatives		Interrogative particles	
Who?	مَنْ	How?	كَيْفَ	Is?	
What?	ما	When?	مَتى	Are?	هَل
What?	ماذا	Whence?	أَيْنَ	Do?	أ
What, which?	أيّ	Why?	لِماذا	Have?	
What, (f) which?	أيّة	How many How much	كَمْ		

VOCABULARY

rajaa' *to return*	رجع - يرجع	baäd al ahyan *sometimes*	بعض الاحيان
kimiya *chemistry*	كيمياء	akar *another*	آخر
adawät *materials*	أدوات : مواد	akir *last*	أخير
adä *tool, instrument*	أداة : آلة	qabl *before*	قبل
bahr *sea; ocean*	بحر	al-än *now*	الآن
shatt *shore, coast*	شط	shaida *to be present; to give testimony*	شهد - يشهد
shati al bahr *seacoast*	شاطئ البحر	ra'ä *to see; observe*	رأى : أبصر
masha *to walk*	مشى - يمشى	marra *once*	مرّة
mashi *pedestrian; cattle*	ماش - ماشية	miräran *several times*	مراراً
ahyanan *occasionally*	أحيانا	jäda *to improve*	جاد : جوّد : حَسَن

sibäha سباحة : عوم
swimming

qasama قسم
to divide, to part

fahima فهم :أدرك
to understand

qisma قسمة
fate, division

istifhäm إستفهام
inquiry, act of inquiring

arafa عرف ـ يعرف
to know

hadata حدث ـ يحدث
to happen

häl حال : حالة
state, condition

haddata حدث ـ روى
to narrate

hamida حمد ـ يحمد
to praise

muhädata محادثة
conversation

alhamdu li Allah الحمد لله
praise be to God

hadit حديث
new, news

ba'du بعد
after, later

bain بين
between

afäda أفاد
to benefit

shaik شيخ
elderly person

fäida فائدة : إفادة
utility, profit

fata فتى ـ شاب
youth

harasa حرس ـ يحرس
to watch

ahlan wa sahlan اهلاً وسهلاً
welcome

häris حارس
watchman

marhaba مرحبا
welcome

akkara أخّر :تأخّر
to delay

ism إسم ـ أسماء
name

mutaakkir متأخر
late

sana سنَة
year

mubakkir مبكراً
early

taallama تَعلّم
to learn

qadä قضى
to spend time, to finish

qism قسم
department, section

shai شيئى :أمر
thing, matter

'inda *with*	عند	jä'a *to come*	جاء : أتى
am : aw *or*	ام : او	tärik *date, history*	تأريخ
iktära *to choose*	إختار : انتخب	walada *to give birth to*	ولد ـ يلد
ba'ata *to send*	بعث ـ يبعث	wulida *to be born*	ولد
bä'it *motive, cause*	باعث	bad'a *to begin*	بدأ : يبدأ
mab'üt *delegate, envoy*	مبعوث : مندوب	utla *leisure, vacation*	عطلة
masä *evening*	مساء	saif *summer*	صيف
yamin *the right hand*	يمين : اليد اليمنى	ujra *hire ; rent ; fee*	أجرة
yasär *the left hand*	يسار : اليد اليسرى	jugrafiya *Geography*	جغرافية
qabila *tribe*	قبيلة : عشيرة	älä *favours*	آلآء
haql *field*	حقل ـ حقول	kadaba *to lie*	كذب ـ يكذب
natija *result, product*	نتيجة : حاصل	kaddaba *to deny*	كذب القول
nataja *to result*	نتج ـ ينتج	taman *price*	ثمن : قيمة
nahwa *side, direction*	نحو	fa'la *to do, perform*	فعل ـ يفعل
qäla *to say*	قال ـ يقول	rabb *lord, master*	رب
qawl *statement*	قول	sahiba *to accompany*	صحب ـ يصحب

Make a note of the interrogatives in the following sentences.

TRANSLATION	MODEL SENTENCES
1. What is that in your right hand, O Moses?	١ . وما تلك بيمينك يا موسى
2. From which tribe are you?	٢ . من أى قبيلة أنت؟
3. Are you hungry?	٣ . أ أنت جائع؟
4. Do you have a watch?	٤ . هل عندك ساعة؟
5. Where is the zoological garden?	٥ . أين حديقة الحيوانات؟
6. How many cows are there in the field?	٦ . كم بقرة فى الحقل؟
7. How many students are there in your school?	٧ . كم تلميذا فى مدرستك؟
8. What is the result of your examination?	٨ . ما نتيجة امتحانك؟
9. What are our duties towards our nation?	٩ . ما واجبنا نحو وطننا؟
10. What did your teacher say?	١٠ . ماذا قال استاذك؟
11. Is your brother in the school?	١١ . هل أخوك فى المدرسة؟
12. Which book is with you?	١٢ . أى كتاب معك؟
13. Why did you go to Delhi?	١٣ . لماذا ذهبت الى دلهى؟
14. When do you return from the college?	١٤ . متى ترجع من الكلية؟
15. How is your health?	١٥ . كيف صحتك؟
16. Then which of the favours of your Lord do you deny?	١٦ . فبأى آلآء ربكما تكذبان؟
17. Why are you travelling?	١٧ . لماذا أنت تسافر؟
18. What is the price of this book?	١٨ . كم ثمن هذا الكتاب؟
19. Did you not see how your Lord dealt with the owners of the elephant?	١٩ . ألم تر كيف فعل ربك بأصحاب الفيل؟

20. Has the news of the army come to you ?	٢٠ . هل أتاك حديث الجنود ؟
21. What is the benefit of iron ?	٢١ . ما فائدة الحديد ؟
22. What is the capital of India ?	٢٢ . ما عاصمة الهند ؟
23. Who are those men ?	٢٣ . مَن هؤلاء الرجال
24. How many days are there in the year ?	٢٤ . كم يوما فى السنة ؟
25. Is the watchman honest ?	٢٥ . هل الحارس أمين ؟
26. When do you play ?	٢٦ . متى تلعب ؟
27. Why are you late ?	٢٧ . لماذا أنت متأخر ؟
28. How did you spend yesterday ?	٢٨ . كيف قضيت أمس ؟
29. What is it that you are having ?	٢٩ . أى شيئى عندك ؟
30. Where is your cycle ?	٣٠ . أين دراجتك ؟
31. When is your examination ?	٣١ . متى إمتحانك
32. What happened yesterday ?	٣٢ . ماذا حدث أمس ؟
33. Did you come walking or riding ?	٣٣ . أماشيا جئت أم راكبا
34. Are you going to Cairo ?	٣٤ . هل أنت ذاهب إلى القاهرة؟
35. What is the date on which you were born ?	٣٥ . ما هو تاريخ اليوم الذى ولدت فيه؟
36. What do the newspapers say about the ministry ?	٣٦ . ماذا تقول الصحف عن الوزارة ؟
37. What is the rent tor this house ?	٣٧ . كم أجرة لهذا البيت ؟
38. What is your age ?	٣٨ . كم عمرك ؟
39. Is your brother in the house or in the school ?	٣٩ . أ أخوك فى البيت أو فى المدرسة ؟
40. When does summer vacation begin ?	٤٠ . متى تبدأ العطلة الصيفية؟

PREPOSITIONS   حـروف الجـر

THE VILLAGE   القـريــة

1. The entire village is full of activity and liveliness and its people are happy.

١. القَريةُ كلها عَمَلٌ ونَشاطٌ واهْلُها فى فَرْحٍ .

2. The peasant is happy with the cultivation of rice.

٢. الفَلّاحُ سَعيدٌ بِزرعِ الارْزِ

3. Because it is an important (source of) income for him and he depends on it.

٣. لانهُ مَحْصُولٌ هامٌّ لهُ ويَعْتَمِدُ عَلَيهِ .

4. He sells it and purchases his requirements out of its price.

٤. يَبيعُهُ ويَشْتَرى حاجتَهُ من ثَمَنِه .

5. The peasant works in the field.

٥. يَعْمَلُ الفَلاحُ فى الحَقْلِ .

6. His sons are at his right and his brother is on his left. His wife is sitting on a rock and with her is the food (packet). And around her are the cattle.

٦. وأبْناؤُهُ عَنْ يَمينِه وأخُوهُ عَن يَسارِه وزَوجَتُهُ جالسَةٌ عَلى صَخْرةٍ وفى يَدِها الطَّعامُ ومِنْ حَولِها البَهائِمُ [المَواشى] .

7. This family is occupied from morning till sun-set.

٧. هذه الاسرةُ تَشْتَغِلُ منَ الصَّباح الى غُرُوبِ الشَّمْسِ .

The preposition is called حــرف الجــر . The word governed by a preposition is called مجــرور and the preposition with its noun is known as الجار والمجــرور

Prepositions are either

(a) Separable e.g. فى *in* (vide sentence No. 1)

(b) Inseparable e.g. ب (in بحرث) *by, with* (vide sentence No. 2)

Nouns followed by prepositions are in the "Genitive Case" i.e. مجــرور They end with ِ which is the sign of the genitive case.

VOCABULARY

fasl *class, season*	فصل	aktubu *I write*	اكتب
ala *high*	على : عال	'amdan *intentional*	عمدا
sufl *low, lowest*	سفل : أسفل	qarya *village*	قرية
tarwa *wealth, riches*	ثروة : غنى	kull *all, whole*	كل
'usfür *a small bird, sparrow*	عصفور : طير	fariha *to be glad*	فرح - يفرح
tävola *table*	طاولة	s'ayeed *lucky, happy*	سعيد
ibta'da *to avoid*	إبتعد ـ يبتعد	urzz *rice*	أرز : رز
katar *danger, risk*	خطر	anna *that*	أن
äda *to return*	عاد : رجع	hasala *to collect*	حصل

mahsul *product, yield*	محصول	jarama *to commit a crime*	جرم
i'tamada *to rely*	اعتمد ـ يعتمد	mujrim *criminal*	مجرم
'imäd *pillar*	عماد	mula'a *fond of, crazy*	مولع
'timäd *reliance*	اعتماد	shafä *to cure*	شفى
la talaab *do not play*	لا تلعب	asir *prisoner*	أسير
när *fire*	نار	bä'a *to sell*	باع ـ يبيع
babgä' *parrot*	ببغاء	bai' *sale, selling*	بيع
qafas *cage*	قفص	ibn *son*	إبن ـ أبناء
hisän *horse*	حصان	bint *daughter*	بنت ـ بنات
afw *pardon*	عفو : عفاء	zawj *husband*	زوج
afwan *I beg your pardon*	عفواً	zawja *wife*	زوجة
fataha *to open*	فتح ـ يفتح	tazawwaja *to marry*	تزوج
miftäh *key*	مفتاح ـ مفاتيح	kullu wahid *each one*	كل واحد
daraj *staircase*	درج	bahima *beasts, animals*	بهيمة ـ بهائم
jä'iza *reward, prize*	جائزة ـ جوائز	usra *family*	أسرة
mustashfa *hospital*	مستشفى	ishtagala *to busy oneself with*	إشتغل

mashgül *busy*	مشغول	safäha *foolishness*	سفاهة : حماقة
sabäh *morning*	صباح	jasad *body*	جسد
gurüb *sunset*	غروب الشمس	mu'ärada *opposition*	معارضة
sajana *to imprison*	سجنَ	sarj *saddle*	سرج
sijn *prison*	سِجن	zahr *back, rear side*	ظهر
sajin *prisoner*	سجين : مسجون	gadiba *to be angry*	غضب ـ يغضب
sayd *hunting*	صيد	gadbän *angry*	غضبان : زعلان
sayyäd *hunter*	صياد : صائد	atä / jäa *to come, arrive*	أتى : جاء
siyäha *tour, journey*	سياحة	basra *Basra*	بصرة
sayyäh *tourist*	سياح	bagdäd *Baghdad*	بغداد
adina *to permit*	أذن : سمح	durj *drawer*	درج
idn *permission*	إذن	sharä *to purchase*	شرى : إشترى
safih *foolish*	سفيه : أحمق	shirä *buying*	شراء

The following sentences contain most of the prepositions.

TRANSLATION	*MODEL SENTENCES*
1. The teacher is in the class.	١ . الاستاذ فى الفصل
2. The upper hand is better than the lower (receiving) hand	٢ . اليد العليا خير من اليد السفلى

3. Knowledge is better than wealth.	٣ . العلم خير من الثروة
4. The sparrow is on the tree.	٤ . العصفور على الشجرة .
5. The book is on the table.	٥ . الكتاب على الطاولة .
6. The wise (person) keeps himself at a distance from danger.	٦ . العاقل يبتعد عن الخطر .
7. The minister returned to the capital.	٧ . عاد الوزير الى العاصمة .
8. I write with my pen.	٨ . أكتب بقلمى .
9. Do not play with fire.	٩ . لا تلعب بالنار .
10. There are two gates for the college and there is a watchman at each.	١٠ . للكلية بابان وعلى كل باب حارس .
11. I saw a parrot in the cage.	١١ . رأيت الببغاء فى القفص .
12. The policeman is getting down from the horse.	١٢ . ينزل الشرطى عن الحصان
13. The generous (person) forgives the wicked.	١٣ . الكريم يعفو عن المسيئى .
14. This key is for my room.	١٤ . هذا المفتاح لغرفتى .
15. The reward is for the winner.	١٥ . الجائزة للسابق .
16. The patient is in the hospital.	١٦ . المريض فى المستشفى .
17. The criminal is in the prison.	١٧ . المجرم فى السجن .
18. The saddle is on the horse's back.	١٨ . السرج على ظهر الفرس .

19. The teacher was angry with the student.

١٩ . غضب الاستاذ على التلميذ

20. Heat comes from the sun.

٢٠ . تأتى الحرارة من الشمس .

21. I travelled from Basra to Baghdad.

٢١ . سافرت من البصرة الى بغداد .

22. He is fond of hunting.

٢٢ . هو مولع بالصيد .

23. The tourist returned to his country.

٢٣ . عاد السياح الى بلده .

24. I hear by my ear.

٢٤ . أسمع باذنى .

25. I differentiated milk from water.

٢٥ . ميزت اللبن عن الماء .

26. Be away from the mischief-makers.

٢٦ . ابتعد عن المفسدين .

"VERBAL" SENTENCE - THE PAST TENSE

الجملة الفعلية ـ الفعل الماضى

SAYEED AND HIS FRIEND	سعيد و صديقه

1. Sayeed returned from the school and placed his bag on the table.

١ . رَجَعَ سَعيدُ مِنَ المَدْرَسَةِ وَ وَضَعَ حَقيبَتَهُ على الطاولةِ .

2. Then he washed his face, took lunch and drank tea.

٢ . ثُمَّ غسَلَ وَجْهَهُ وتَنَاوَلَ وجْبَةَ الغَداءِ وشَرِبَ الشاى .

3. He went out of the house for recreation and reached the house of his friend, William.

٣ . وخَرَجَ مِنَ البَيْتِ للنُّزْهَةِ ووَصَلَ إلى مَنْزِلِ صَديقِهِ «وليم» .

4. Then the two friends went to the industrial exhibition and witnessed a variety of Indian products. They (two) returned after purchasing some items (things).

٤ . ثُمَّ ذَهَبَ الصَّديقانِ إلى المَعْرَضِ الصِّناعى وشاهدا انواعا مِنَ المُنْتَجاتِ الهنديةِ وعادا بَعْدَ أن إشْتَرَيا بعض الاشياء .

5. But Sayeed's sister went to the kitchen and helped her mother in cooking.

٥ . لكن ذَهَبَتْ أختُ سعيد إلى المطبخ وسَاعَدَتْ أمَّها فى الطَّبَخِ .

6. Her father returned from the market and in his hand was a basket full of vegetables and fruits.

٦ . ورَجَعَ ابوها مِنَ السُّوقِ وفى يَده سَلَّةٌ مَمْلوءَةٌ بِالخَضَرِ والفاكِهة .

7. Zainab saw her father and she hurried towards him and took the basket from him.

٧. رَأَتْ زينب أَباها فأَسْرَعَتْ إِلَيه وأَخذَتِ السَّلَّةَ مِنْهُ.

8. The father was happy with Zainab for her love for him.

٨. فَرِحَ الأَبُ بِزَينب لحُبِّها لهُ.

9. The mother brought supper and all of them sat around the dining table. The family took supper and thanked God for His bounty.

٩. وأَحْضَرَتِ الامُّ العَشَاء فَجَلَسُوا جَمِيعا حَولَ المائِدَةِ وتَناوَلَتِ الاسرَةُ العَشاء وشَكَرُوا اللّهَ عَلى نِعَمِهِ.

VERB : AN INTRODUCTION

A sentence which begins with a verb is called الجملة الفعلية "The verbal sentence". The verb consists of three root or radical letters e.g. فعل *to do* كتب *to write*. These are called triliteral verbs. But there are some quadriliteral verbs too, like دحرج *to push*, which consist of four radical letters.

To know the radical letters of any given verb is essential in order to find its meaning in the Arabic dictionaries. Take for instance the word فعل which consists of (1) ف, (2) ع, and (3) ل.

(1)ف is called كلمة الفاء the first radical

(2) ع is called كلمة العين the second radical

(3) ل is called كلمة اللام the third radical

(The three radicals are derived from المصدر the verb root)

Remember that in all books of Arabic Grammar, the verb فعل and its derivatives are used as patterns for all verbs whether triliteral or quadriliteral and their derivatives.

In Arabic dictionaries, a verb in the form of the 3rd person, singular masculine, simple perfect, and in the active voice, is given first and its derivatives down below. Further the meaning given would be in the infinite

e.g. *to do* for فعل *to see* for نظر whereas the actual meaning of فعل is *he did* and that of نظر *he saw*.

The Arab Grammarians have divided the verbs into three categories:

(1) the Perfect denoting a completed action   الفعل الماضى

(2) the Imperfect denoting an incomplete action   الفعل المضارع

(3) the Imperative (which includes the Negative)   الفعل الأمر

AGREEMENT BETWEEN THE VERB AND THE SUBJECT:

The principal rules relating to the agreement between فعل *verb* and its فاعل *subject* are as follows:

(a) when the فعل *verb* precedes the subject:

(1) If the فاعل *subject* is masculine singular, or dual or plural, the verb is put in the 3rd person singular masculine.

e.g. Sayeed returned	رجع سعيد
The two friends went	ذهب الصديقان
(Many) men went	ذهب الرجال

(2) If the فاعل *subject* is feminine singular, or dual or plural the verb is put in the 3rd person singular feminine.

e.g. Sayeed's sister went	ذهبت أخت سعيد
The two girls went	ذهبت البنتان
Many girls went	ذهبت البنات

(3) If الفاعل *the subject* is a collective noun, the verb may be in the 3rd person singular, masculine or feminine.

e.g. The family took supper تناولت الاسرة طعام العشاء

(b) If الفاعل *the subject* comes before الفعل *the verb,* the verb must agree with it in gender and number.

e.g. The two friends witnessed	الصديقان شاهدا
Many boys witnessed	الاولاد شاهدوا
Many girls witnessed	البنات شاهدن

Vowels of the second radical:

In the active voice, the first and the third radicals of verbs in the past tense, will have ﹷ, while the second radical may have either of the three vowel signs ﹷ ﹻ ﹹ These three types of verbs are illustrated below:

نَصَرَ	ضَرَبَ	جَلَسَ	دَخَلَ	فَتَحَ	١ . فَعَلَ
to help	to strike	to sit	to enter	to open	

لَبِسَ	شَهِدَ	حَسِبَ	سَمِعَ	شَرِبِ	٢ . فَعِلَ
to wear	to see	to suppose	to hear	to drink	

ضَعُفَ	كَبُرَ	قَرُبَ	بَعُدَ	كَرُمَ	٣ . فَعُلَ
to grow weak	to grow	to be near	to be distant	to be generous	

NOTE : When a verb in the past tense is converted into the future tense, the vowel of the second radical remains the same in the case of some verbs, and changes in respect of others.

Conjugation of the Past Tense:

					suffixes		3rd Per. Mas.
كَرُمَ	سَمِعَ	نَصَرَ		He did		١ . فَعَلَ	Sing.
كَرُما	سَمِعا	نَصَرا	١	They two did		٢ . فَعَلَا	Dual
كَرُمُوا	سَمِعُوا	نَصَرُوا	وا	They did		٣ . فَعَلُوا	Plural

3rd Per. Fem.

		English	Suffix	نَصَرَ	سَمِعَ	كَرُمَ
٤ Sing.	فَعَلَتْ	She did	تْ	نَصَرَتْ	سَمِعَتْ	كَرُمَتْ
٥ Dual	فَعَلَتَا	They two did	تَا	نَصَرَتَا	سَمِعَتَا	كَرُمَتَا
٦ Plural	فَعَلْنَ	They did	نَ	نَصَرْنَ	سَمِعْنَ	كَرُمْنَ

2nd Per. Mas.

		English	Suffix	نَصَرَ	سَمِعَ	كَرُمَ
٧ Sing.	فَعَلْتَ	You did	تَ	نَصَرْتَ	سَمِعْتَ	كَرُمْتَ
٨ Dual	فَعَلْتُما	You two did	تُما	نَصَرْتُما	سَمِعْتُما	كَرُمْتُما
٩ Plural	فَعَلْتُمْ	you (all) did	تُمْ	نَصَرْتُمْ	سَمِعْتُمْ	كَرُمْتُمْ

2nd Per. Fem.

		English	Suffix	نَصَرَ	سَمِعَ	كَرُمَ
١٠ Sing.	فَعَلْتِ	You did	تِ	نَصَرْتِ	سَمِعْتِ	كَرُمْتِ
١١ Dual	فَعَلْتُما	You two did	تُما	نَصَرْتُما	سَمِعْتُما	كَرُمْتُما
١٢ Plural	فَعَلْتُنَّ	You (all) did	تُنَّ	نَصَرْتُنَّ	سَمِعْتُنَّ	كَرُمْتُنَّ

1st Per. Mas / Fem.

		English	Suffix	نَصَرَ	سَمِعَ	كَرُمَ
١٣ Sing.	فَعَلْتُ	I did	ثُ	نَصَرْتُ	سَمِعْتُ	كَرُمْتُ

1st Per. Mas / Fem.

		English	Suffix	نَصَرَ	سَمِعَ	كَرُمَ
١٤ Plural	فَعَلْنا	We did	نا	نَصَرْنا	سَمِعْنا	كَرُمْنا

الماضى القريب "The Near Past" is formed by the addition of قد to
الفعل الماضى

e.g.   *He has gone*   قَدْ ذَهَبَ

         He has heard   قَدْ سَمِعَ

The past negative is formed by adding ما to the past tense.

e.g.   *He did not go*   ما ذَهَبَ

         He did not hear   ما سَمِعَ

1. The Verb, like the personal pronouns, has three persons:

   1. First person, *the speaker*   المتكلم

   2. Second person, *the individual spoken to*   المخاطب

   3. Third person, *the individual spoken of*   الغائب

2. The endings in the conjugation are simply shortened forms of personal pronouns used as nominative.

3. When a personal pronoun is the direct object of a verb it is attached to it as a suffix.

e.g.   *I love you.*   أُحِبُّكَ

         I sent them out.   أَخْرَجْتُهم

4. A peculiar feature of the Arabic language is its comprehensiveness. What is conveyed in a sentence in other languages, is sometimes expressed in a word in Arabic. (see above)

VOCABULARY

akada	أخذ ـ يأخذ	haqiba	حقيبة
to take, receive		*bag*	
ahdara	أحضر : جاء به	ashä	عَشاء
to bring, fetch		*dinner, supper*	
wadaa	وضع ـ يضع	gadä	غَداء : طعام الظهر
to put, to place		*lunch*	

futūr *breakfast*	فطور : أكل الصباح	igtasala *to bathe*	إغتسل ـ يغتسل
jami'an *all, entirely*	جميعا : الكل	wajh *face*	وجه ـ وجوه
tanāwala *to take food*	تناول الطعام	shāy *tea*	شاى
nāla *to obtain*	نال ـ ينال	karaja *to go*	خرج ـ يخرج
shakara *to thank*	شكر ـ يشكر	nuzha *excursion, recreation*	نزهة
ahd ashar *eleven*	أحد عشر	wasala *to reach*	وصل ـ يصل
gādara *to depart*	غادر ـ يغادر	manzil *residence*	منزل : دار : بيت
qitār *train*	قطار	m'rad *exhibition*	معرض
bā'i *seller, merchant*	بائع	arada *to display, to offer*	عرض ـ يعرض
ma'bad *place of worship*	معبد	nau' *variety, sort*	نوع ـ انواع
matbak *kitchen*	مطبخ	tabaka *to cook food*	طبخ الطعام
dakara *to remember, to mention*	ذكر	tabbāk *cook*	طباخ
da'ā *to call*	دعا : نادى	sä'da *to help, to assist*	ساعد
da'wa *invitation, propaganda*	دعوة	süq *market*	سوق ـ اسواق
hafala *to gather*	حفل	salla *basket*	سلة

sallat - almuhmalät سلة المهملات
waste paper basket

zamil زميل ـ زملآء
companion, colleague

hafla حفلة
meeting

dawä' دواء ـ أُدوية
medicine

haflat al - shäy حفلة الشاى
tea party

mamlü' مملوء
filled up, loaded

harasa حرس
to watch, to guard

fajr فجر
dawn

häris حارس
watchman

harb حرب
war

bädat باضت الدجاجة
the hen laid eggs

satr سطر
line, row

baida بيضة ـ بيض
egg

sura' سرعة
haste

nabaha نبج ـ ينبج
to bark

asra' أسرع
hurry

kalb كلب ـ كلاب
dog

dajjäja دجاجة
hen

'amid عميد
principal

arsala أرسل ـ يرسل
to send, to forward

liss لص : سارق
thief

rasül رسول
messenger, envoy

tallaqa طلق
to leave, to divorce

risäla رسالة ـ خطاب
message, letter

atlaqa أطلق
to release, to free

iltaqata إلتقط ـ يلتقط
to pick up

a'düw عدو ـ أعداء
enemy

finä ad - där فناء الدار
courtyard

rihla رحلة
excursion, journey

näfida نافذة : شباك
window

aäsha *to live*	عاش	kura *ball, globe*	كرة
tägür *Tagore*	تاغور	aglaqa *to close*	أغلق
bengäl *Bengal*	بنغال	rahala *to depart, leave*	رحل
hiläl *crescent*	هلال	säha ad-dik *cock's crow*	صاح الديك
säha *to call*	صاح : نادى	allaqa *to attach*	علق
deek *cock*	ديك	jarra *to pull*	جر ـ يجر
shammäa *hat and clothes rack*	شماعة	mubärä *match, contest*	مباراة : مسابقة
mihrät *plough*	محراث : آلة الحرث	kuratu al-qadam *football*	كرة القدم

Observe the use of the verb, in the Past tense in the following sentences:

TRANSLATION	MODEL SENTENCES
1. I saw eleven stars	١ . رأيت أحد عشر كوكبا .
2. Marwan has written his lesson.	٢ . قد كتب مروان درسه .
3. The peasant went to the field.	٣ . ذهب الفلاح الى الحقل .
4. The Minister has left Delhi.	٤ . قد غادر الوزير دهلى .
5. The teacher (f) reached Madras by the train.	٥ . وصلت المعلمة مدراس بالقطار .
6. The seller (f) of the flowers sat at the door of the temple.	٦ . جلست بائعة الازهار على باب المعبد .

7. I remembered my friend who travelled to Egypt.

٧ . ذكرت صديقى الذى سافر إلى مصر .

8. I invited my friends to a tea party.

٨ . دعوت أصدقائى لحفلة الشاى .

9. The watchman placed the key in its place.

٩ . وضع الحارس المفتاح فى مكانه .

10. Rain descended from the sky.

١٠ . نزل المطر من السماء .

11. The gardener plucked the rose.

١١ . قطف البستانى الوردة .

12. The hen laid egg.

١٢ . باضت الدجاجة .

13. Khalid sent a letter to his people.

١٣ . أرسل خالد رسالة إلى أهله .

14. Mahatma Gandhi had struggled for the independence of India.

١٤ . قد جاهد مهاتما غاندى لاستقلال الهند .

15. The student took the paper from the compound of the school and put it in the wastepaper basket.

١٥ . إلتقط التلميذ ورقة من فناء المدرسة ووضعها فى سلة المهملات .

16. The girls have passed in the examination.

١٦ . البنات نجحن فى الامتحان .

17. The girl ate the apple.

١٧ . أكلت البنت التفاحة .

18. The peasant cultivated sugar-cane

١٨ . زرع الفلاح قصب السكر .

19. Tagore lived in Bengal.

١٩ . عاش تاغور فى بنغال .

20. I listened to the advice of my teacher.	٢٠ . سمعت نصيحة أُستاذى .
21. The dog barked at the thief.	٢١ . نبح الكلب على اللص .
22. The student opened his book.	٢٢ . فتح التلميذ كتابه .
23. The Principal has returned from abroad.	٢٣ . قد عاد العميد من الخارج .
24. The soldier opened fire on the enemy.	٢٤ . أطلق الجندى النار على العدو .
25. Towfeek went for excursion with his classmates.	٢٥ . خرج توفيق فى رحلة مع زملائه .
26. The sickman asked the nurse for medicine.	٢٦ . طلب المريض الدواء من الممرضة .
27. The crescent appeared on the sky.	٢٧ . ظهر الهلال فى السماء .
28. The cock crew at dawn.	٢٨ . صاح الديك فى الفجر .
29. Jowhar hung his clothes on the hanger.	٢٩ . علق جوهر ملابسه على الشماعة .
30. The two bulls pulled the plough.	٣٠ . جر الثوران المحراث .
31. My brother witnessed the football match.	٣١ . شاهد أخى مباراة كرة القدم .
32. The boy closed the windows.	٣٢ . أغلق الولد النوافذ .

LESSON SIXTEEN

PRESENT AND FUTURE TENSE

THE IMPERFECT TENSE

الفعل المضارع

God's Deputy

خليفة الله [آيات من القرآن]

1. How do you disbelieve God? When you were dead, He gave life to you. Then He will cause you to die and bring you to life again. And then you shall return to Him.

١ . كَيْفَ تَكْفُرُونَ باللهِ وَكُنْتُمْ أَمْواتا فَأَحْياكُمْ ثُمَّ يُمِيتُكُمْ ثُمَّ يُحْيِيكُمْ ثُمَّ إِلَيْهِ تُرْجَعُونَ .

2. It is He who created for you all that is on the earth. Then He turned to the heaven and fashioned it as seven heavens (skies). And He has knowledge of all things.

٢ . هُوَ الَّذِى خَلَقَ لَكُمْ ما فِى الارضِ جَمِيعاً ثُمَّ اسْتَوى إلى السَّماءِ فَسَوَّاهُنَّ سَبْعَ سَمواتٍ وَهُوَ بِكُل شَيْىءٍ عَلِيُمْ .

3. And when your Lord said to the angels "I am about to create a deputy on the earth," they replied: "Will you place therein one who will do harm there and shed blood? And we do celebrate your praises and glorify your holy (names)". He said: "Surely I know that which you do not know."

٣ . وَإِذْ قَالَ رَبُّكَ لِلْمَلَئِكَةِ إِنِّى جاعِلٌ فِى الارضِ خَلِيفَةً قالُوا أَتَجْعَلُ فِيها مَنْ يُفْسِدُ فِيها وَيَسْفِكُ الدِّماءَ وَنَحْنُ نُسَبِّحُ بِحَمْدِكَ وَنُقَدِّسُ لَكَ قال إِنِّى أَعْلَمُ مالا تَعْلَمُونَ .

PRESENT AND FUTURE TENSES *(The Imperfect)* الفعل المضارع

The Imperfect tense, الفعل المضارع expresses an action still incomplete and could mean either (1) Present and Present continuous tenses or (2) Future Imperfect tense. The Imperfect tense is made from the three radical letters of the past tense الفعل الماضى and with the addition of one or more of these letters :- ى ، ن ، ت ، ا . These are known as "the signs of the Imperfect tense". From كتب *he wrote* (past tense) the following Imperfect tenses are formed : e.g.

نَكْتُبُ	اُكْتُبُ	يَكْتُبُ	تَكْتُبُ
We are writing or will write.	I am writing or will write.	He writes or will write.	You are writing or will write.

You would note that the first radical letter of the Imperfect verb has no vowel mark, but is governed by the vowel of the sign of مضارع

The number and gender of the person is expressed in the conjugation with the addtion of ا ، ت ، ن ، ى

The Imperfect الفعل المضارع in itself denotes only unfinished action, but it may be made to indicate the future by putting the independent word سوف before it, or by prefixing its contraction : (سـ) س :

e.g. Zaid is writing or will write.   يكتب زيد

Zaid will write. [in future] سوف يكتب زيد   سيكتب زيد

س is used to indicate "near future" and سوف is used for "distant future".

The vowel of 2nd radical of the Imperfect, would in respect of some verbs, be the same as that of the past perfect, e.g.

Imperfect		Past	
يَفْتَحُ	to open	فَتَحَ	١ .
يَكْرُمُ	to be generous	كَرُمَ	٢ .
يَحْسِبُ	to suppose	حَسِبَ	٣ .

But in some verbs, the vowel of the 2nd radical of the Imperfect, المضارع is different from that of the second radical of the past perfect الماضى*

e.g.	Imperfect		Past	
	يَسْمَعُ	to hear	سَمِعَ	٤.
	يَنْصُرُ	to help	نَصَرَ	٥.
	يَضْرِبُ	to strike	ضَرَبَ	٦.

The vowel of 2nd radical of the imperfect is always shown in the dictionaries along with the meaning of the past perfect verb. The conjugation of the model verbs, given above, is as follows :

CONJUGATION OF THE IMPERFECT TENSE

غائب مذكر

3rd Per. Mas.

Sing.

يَضْرِبُ يَنْصُرُ يَسْمَعُ يَحْسِبُ يَكْرُمُ يَفْتَحُ

Dual

يَضْرِبانِ يَنْصُرَانِ يَسْمَعَانِ يَحْسِبانِ يَكْرُمانِ يَفْتَحَانِ

Plural

يَضْرِبُونَ يَنْصُرُونَ يَسْمَعُونَ يَحْسِبُونَ يَكْرُمُونَ يَفْتَحُونَ

غائب مؤنث

3rd Per. Fem.

Sing.

تَضْرِبُ تَنْصُرُ تَسْمَعُ تَحْسِبُ تَكْرُمُ تَفْتَحُ

---

*Whenever 1st, 2nd and 3rd radicals are mentioned, they refer to the three radicals of the triliteral verbs, which are derived from the verb root (vide page: 80).

Dual

تُفْتَحانِ تُكْرُمانِ تُحْسِبانِ تُسْمَعانِ تُنْصُرانِ تُضْرِبانِ

Plural

يَفْتَحْنَ يَكْرُمْنَ يَحْسِبْنَ يَسْمَعْنَ يَنْصُرْنَ يَضْرِبْنَ

مخاطب مذكر

2nd Per. Mas.

Sing.

تَفْتَحُ تَكْرُمُ تَحْسِبُ تَسْمَعُ تَنْصُرُ تَضْرِبُ

Dual

تَفْتَحان تَكْرُمانِ تَحْسِبانِ تَسْمَعانِ تَنْصُرانِ تَضْرِبانِ

Plural

تَفْتَحُونَ تَكْرُمُونَ تَحْسِبُونَ تَسْمَعُونَ تَنْصُرُونَ تَضْرِبُونَ

مخاطب مؤنث

2nd Per. Fem.

Sing.

تَفْتَحِينَ تَكْرُمِينَ تَحْسِبِينَ تَسْمَعِينَ تَنْصُرِينَ تَضْرِبِينَ

Dual

تَفْتَحان تَكْرُمانِ تَحْسِبانِ تَسْمَعانِ تَنْصُرانِ تَضْرِبانِ

Plural

تَفْتَحْنَ تَكْرُمْنَ تَحْسِبْنَ تَسْمَعْنَ تَنْصُرْنَ تَضْرِبْنَ

متكلم مذكر مؤنث

1st Per. Mas. / Fem. Sing.

أَفْتَحُ اَكْرُمُ اَحْسِبُ اَسْمَعُ اَنْصُرُ اَضْرِبُ

نَفْتَحُ نَكْرُمُ نَحْسِبُ نَسْمَعُ نَنْصُرُ نَضْرِبُ

VOCABULARY

sära *to go, to be in motion*	نَسار ـ يسير	hayy *alive*	حيّ
sair *walk, march*	سير	ahyä *to give life*	أحيا
sahrä *desert*	صحراء	istawa *to straighten*	إستوى
ajjala *to hasten*	عجل : إستعجل	sawwa *to level, to arrange*	سوّى
aajal *haste, speed*	عجل : سرعة	fäza *to triumph*	فاز ـ يفوز
nadima *to repent*	ندم ـ يندم	fauz *success, victory*	فوز : ظفر
nädim *repentant*	نادم	qamh *wheat*	قمح
di'b *wolf, jackal*	ذئب	hawä' *air, atmosphere*	هواء
kafara *to deny, to be ungrateful*	كفر ـ يكفر	tamattu' *enjoyment*	تمتع
käna *to be, to happen*	كان ـ يكون	matana *firmness*	متانة
mäta *to die*	مات ـ يموت	saqata *to fall down*	سقط ـ يسقط
mawt *death*	موت	talläja *refrigerator*	ثلاجة : مثلجة
shitä' *winter*	شتاء	kalifa *deputy, vicegerent, caliph*	خليفة

idäa *broadcast*	إذاعة : الاخبار	afsada *to spoil, to corrupt*	أفسد ـ يفسد
rädiyo *radio*	راديو	fasäd *corruption*	فساد
musäada *assistance, help, aid*	مساعدة : معاونة	safaka *to shed (blood)*	سفك ـ يسفك
nasara *to help*	نصر ـ ينصر	dam *blood*	دم ـ دماء
salla *to pray*	صلى ـ يصلى	sabbaha *to praise, to glorify*	سبح ـ يسبح
salä *prayer*	صلوة	tasbih *praise of God*	تسبيح : حمد
wafd *a delegation*	وفد	qaddasa *to sanctify, to glorify*	قدس ـ يقدس
shahr *month*	شهر	muqaddis *holy, reverent*	مقدس : متقدس
saba *seven*	سبع	samak *fish*	سمك
id *then*	إذ	musäwama *bargaining*	مساومة
malik *king*	ملك	qädim *arriving*	قادم : مقبل
ja'la *to make, to create*	جعل ـ يجعل	ash-shahr alqädim *the next month*	الشهر القادم
jä'l *maker*	جاعل	farräsh *office boy*	فراش

nuzha	نزهة	karif	خريف
pleasure trip		*autumn*	
halaba	حلب : إستحلب	ishtadda	إشتد
to milk		*to grow severe, violent*	
qäfila	قافلة	bakä	بكى - يبكى
caravan		*to weep*	
siyäda	سيادة	mahd	مهد
his excellency, rule		*cradle*	
safina	سفينة : مركب	firäsh	فِراش
boat, ship		*bed*	

Observe the use of the verb in the Imperfect Tense in the following sentences.

TRANSLATION	*MODEL SENTENCES*
1. The boys are playing with the ball.	١ . يلعب الاولاد بالكرة .
2. Fish lives in water.	٢ . يعيش السمك فى الماء
3. Rain descends from the sky.	٣ . ينزل المطر من السماء .
4. The sun rises from the east.	٤ . تطلع الشمس من المشرق .
5. Mahmood is purchasing the pen.	٥ . يشترى محمود القلم .
6. The boat is floating on the water.	٦ . تجرى السفينة فى الماء .
7. We will take a walk (for recreation) in the garden.	٧ . سوف نتنزه فى الحدائق .
8. The boy will swim in the river.	٨ . سوف يسبح الغلام فى النهر
9. The leaves of the trees fall in autumn.	٩ . تسقط أوراق الاشجار فى الخريف .

10. Heat becomes severe in summer.	١٠ . يشتد الحر فى الصيف .
11. The merchant is selling the furniture.	١١ . يبيع التاجر الاثاث .
12. The child is weeping in the cradle.	١٢ . يبكى الطفل فى المهد .
13. A trade delegation from Iraq will reach New Delhi tomorrow.	١٣ . يصل إلى دلهى الجديدة غدا وفد تجارى من العراق .
14. His Excellency the Ambassador of Saudi Arabian Kingdom will visit Madras next month.	١٤ . سيزور سيادة سفير المملكة العربية السعودية مدراس فى الشهر القادم .
15. I am sending my salutations to you.	١٥ . أبلغ سلامى اليك .
16. I will spend the spring in Kashmir.	١٦ . أقضى الربيع فى كشمير .
17. Caravan(s) pass in the desert of Arabia.	١٧ . تسير القوافل بصحراء العرب
18. One who makes haste will repent.	١٨ . من يستعجل يندم .
19. Children are afraid of the wolf.	١٩ . يخاف الاطفال من الذئب .
20. Fowzia understands her lesson.	٢٠ . تفهم فوزية درسها .
21. The peasant cultivates wheat.	٢١ . يزرع الفلاح القمح .
22. The wind enters the room.	٢٢ . يدخل الهواء فى الحجرة .
23. The girl is cleaning the clothes.	٢٣ . تنظف البنت الثياب .

24. The woman cooked the food.

٢٤ . طبخت المرأة الطعام .

25. The girl milked the cow.

٢٥ . حلبت الفتاة البقرة .

26. Snow falls in winter.

٢٦ . يسقط الثلج شتاء .

27. You will hear an important announcement on the Radio.

٢٧ . سوف تسمعون اعلانا هاما من المذياع (راديو) .

28. I am seeking your help.

٢٨ . أطلب مساعدتك .

29. We ask for God's help.

٢٩ . نستعين بالله .

30. We start our day with prayer.

٣٠ . نفتتح يومنا بالصلاة .

THE IMPERATIVE AND THE NEGATIVE COMMAND

فعل الامـر و النـهـى

LUQMAN'S SERMON

وعظ لقمـان

1. Read : With the name of your Lord Who created ; created man from a clot.

١ . إقْرَأْ بِاسْمِ رَبِّكَ الَّذِى خَلَقَ خَلَقَ الاِنْسَانَ مِنْ عَلَقٍ .

2. Read : And your Lord is Most Generous, Who taught by the pen, taught man that which he did not know.

٢ . إقْرَأْ وَرَبُّكَ الاكْرَمُ الَّذِى عَلَّمَ بِالْقَلَمِ عَلَّمَ الاِنْسَانَ مَا لَمْ يَعْلَمْ .

3. And when Luqman said to his son, by way of instruction : "O my son! Do not associate (any thing) with God in His worship. Indeed false worship is a tremendous wrong.

٣ . وإذْ قَالَ لُقْمَانُ لِابْنِهِ وَهُوَ يَعِظُهُ يَا بُنَيَّ لاتُشْرِكْ بِاللهِ إنَّ الشِّرْكَ لَظُلْمٌ عَظِيمٌ .

4. O my son! Be steadfast in prayer, ask (people) to do good things and forbid (them) from abominable things, and patiently bear whatever misfortune falls upon you, for this is the firmness (of purpose) in (the conduct of) affairs. Do not turn your cheek in scorn against people. Do not walk the land proudly ; for God does not love arrogant boasters.

٤ . يَا بُنَيَّ أقِمِ الصَّلوةَ وَأمُرْ بِالْمَعْرُوفِ وَانْهَ عَنِ الْمُنْكَرِ وَاصْبِرْ عَلَى ما أصَابَكَ إنَّ ذلِكَ مِنْ عَزْمِ الأُمُورِ ولا تُصَعِّرْ خَدَّكَ لِلنَّاسِ وَلاتَمْشِ فِى الارضِ مَرَحاً إنَّ اللهَ لا يُحِبُّ كُلَّ مُخْتَالٍ فَخُورٍ .

5. Be modest in your bearing (pace) and lower your voice; for the harshest of all sounds is the braying of the ass".

٥ . وَاقْصِدْ فِى مَشْيِكَ وَاغْضُضْ مِنْ صَوْتِكَ إِنَّ أَنْكَرَ الاصْوَاتِ لَصَوْتُ الْحَمِيرِ .

THE IMPERATIVES:

The Imperative, فعل الآمر is formed from المضارع المخاطب im-perfect 2nd person. Rules for making the Imperative are as follows:

1. If the letter after the sign of مضارع is with the vowel sign, drop the sign of مضارع, and give ـْ to the last letter: e.g.

تَعِدُ ـ عِدْ   تَزِنُ ـ زِنْ   تَضَعُ ـ ضَعْ

you promise   *you weigh*   *you put*

2. If the letter, after the sign of مضارع is without the vowel sign, add "hamza" أ in the beginning, after dropping the sign of مضارع and give ـْ to the last letter.

(a) Then look at the vowel of the 2nd radical. If it is ـُ give the same to أ "the hamzat al wasal" : e.g.

تَنْصُرُ ـ أُنْصُرْ   تَكْرُمُ ـ أُكْرُمْ   تَقْرُبُ ـ أُقْرُبْ

you help   *you honour*   *you come near*

(b) But if the second radical has ـَ or ـِ as its vowel, then give ـِ to أ "the hamzat al wasal" : e.g.

تَصْرِفُ ـ إِصْرِفْ   تَضْرِبُ ـ إِضْرِبْ   تَحْسِبُ ـ إِحْسِبْ

you spend   *you strike*   *you suppose*

تَشْرُبُ ـ إِشْرَبْ   تَسْمَعُ ـ إِسْمَعْ   تَذْهَبُ ـ إِذْهَبْ

you drink   *you hear*   *you go*

3. Further after adopting the above procedure, if any of the "weak letters", ا, و, ى are found at the end, they are dropped. So is ن which is used as a vowel.

THE NEGATIVE COMMAND :

The positive command is changed into a negative command by prefixing لا to المضارع المخاطب *Imperfect 2nd person*. Further the last letter is made vowelless. e.g.

Do not grieve لاتَحْزَنْ ــ تَحْزَنُ   *Do not fear* تَخافُ ــ لاتَخَفْ

Conjugation of the Imperative and Negative command

فعل الامر والنـ ٥

2nd person Mas.

اِفْعَلْ	عِدْ	اُنْصُرْ	اِحْسِبْ	اُدْعُ	لاتَفْعَلْ	Sing.
اِفْعَلا	عِدا	اُنْصُرا	اِحْسِبا	اُدْعُوا	لاتَفْعَلا	dual
اِفْعَلُوا	عِدُوا	اُنْصُرُوا	اِحْسِبُوا	اُدْعُوا	لاتَفْعَلُوا	plural

2nd person Fem.

اِفْعَلِى	عِدِى	اُنْصُرى	اِحْسِبِى	اُدْعِى	لاتَفْعَلِى	Sing.
اِفْعَلا	عِدَا	اُنْصُرَا	اِحْسِبا	اُدْعُوَا	لاتَفْعَلَا	dual
اِفْعَلْنَ	عِدْنَ	اُنْصُرْنَ	اِحْسِبْنَ	اُدْعِينَ	لاتَفْعَلْنَ	plural

VOCABULARY

azm al umür	عزم الامور	iqra'	اِقرأ
firmness of purpose		*you read*	
azama ala	عزم على	qara'	قرأ ــ يقرأ
to resolve upon, to determine		*to read*	
akram	أكرم	amr	أمر ــ أمور
most generous		*matter, affair*	

sa'ira صعر وجهه
to be awry (face with pride)

lä tusa'ir لاتصعر
Do not turn in scorn

luqmän لقمان
luqman

'allama علم ـ يعلم
to teach

kadd خد
cheek

wa'aza وعظ ـ يعظ
to preach, to advise

maraha مرحا
proudly, hilarious

shirk شرك
polytheism

katala ختل : خدع
to deceive

zulm ظلم
injustice, oppression

fakür فخور
proud, boasting

zalama ظلم ـ يظلم
to wrong, to oppress

fakara فخر
to be proud

zälim ظالم
unjust, tyrant

iqtasada fi إقتصد فى
to economise, to be moderate

mazlüm مظلوم
innocent, oppressed

gadda غض : خفض
to lower

aqäma أقام ـ يقيم
to establish, to reside

saut صوت ـ أصوات
vote, noise

amara أمر ـ يامر
to order, instruct

himär حمار ـ حمير
donkey

nahä نهى ـ ينهى
to prohibit, forbid

sakira سخر
to ridicule, utilize

ma'rüf معروف ـ احسان
recognised, good

'asä عسى : لعل
may be, perhaps

qaum قوم : شعب
people, nation

ahsana أحسن
to do well

munkar منكر
an abomination, forbidden

'alaq علق
clot, blood clot

sabara صبر ـ يصبر
to be patient

manzil *dwelling place*	منزل : مثوى	sidq *truth*	صدق : حق : حقيقة
nazzafa *to clean*	نظف ـ ينظف	asäba *to befall, to happen*	أصابت(المصيبة)
rattaba *to arrange*	رتب ـ يرتب	musiba *misfortune, calamity*	مصيبة
da'if *weak*	ضعيف ـ ضعفاء	gair *other than, another*	غير ـ آخر
abr *crossing*	عبر ـ عبور	tajassasa *to spy, to explore*	تجسس
taraka *to leave, quit*	ترك ـ يترك	jäsüs *spy*	جاسوس ـ جواسيس
sunbür *tap*	صنبور : حنفية	ba'd *some, part*	بعض
ramä *to throw*	رمى ـ يرمى	ba'dukum ba'dan *each other*	بعضكم بعضا
hahib *fearful*	رهيب	bugd *hatred*	بنض
ihmäl *negligence*	إهمال ـ تهامل	isti'mär *colonialism*	إستعمار
ahmala *to neglect*	أهمل ـ يهمل	musä *Moses*	موسى
näma *to sleep*	نام ـ ينام	härün *Aron*	هرون
istaiqaza *to wake up*	إستيقظ ـ يستيقظ	firaun *Pharaoh*	فرعون
ihtarama *to respect*	إحترم ـ يحترم	taga *to trespass, to tyrannise*	طغى
hafiza *to memorise, to protect*	حفظ ـ يحفظ	ni'ma *blessing, gift*	نعمة : منة

ämana bi	آمن به	akkara	أخر
to believe in		to delay	
mu'min	مؤمن	la'lla	لعل
believer, faithful		perhaps	
sallama	سلم على : حيا	tadakkara	تذكر
to salute, greet		to keep in mind, to think of	
katura	كثر ـ يكثر	tatawwur	تطور
to do much		development, progress	
sharir	شرير : ردى	waqafa	وقف ـ يقف
wicked, bad		to stop	
qishr	قشر	nataqa	نطق ـ ينطق
peal, crust		to utter	
tabdir	تبذير	ishara - tul - murür	إشارة المرور
squandering, waste		traffic signal	
lubäb	لباب	marra	مر ـ يمر
marrow, best part		to pass by, proceed	
miskin	مسكين	igtiyäb	إغتياب
needy, poor		slander, defamation	
tadkira	تذكرة ـ تذاكر	ibnas - sabil	إبن السبيل
ticket, note		wayfarer	

Observe the use of the verb in the imperative and negative forms in the following sentences :

TRANSLATION	*MODEL SENTENCES*
1. Be kind towards the orphans, the disabled and the wayfarer.	١ . إرحم اليتامى و المساكين وابن السبيل .
2. Let not people ridicule others, who perhaps may be better than themselves.	٢ . لا يسخر قوم من قوم عسى أن يكونوا خيرا منهم

3. Do not call those who are slain in the way of God as dead. But they are living.

٣ . ولا تقولوا لمن يُقتل فى سبيل الله اموات بل احياء

4. God said to Moses and Aron "Go, both of you, to Pharoah, certainly he has transgressed (the bounds)."

٤ . قال الله لموسى وهرون إذهبا إلى فرعون إنه طغى .

5. Remember (all of you) the favour of God upon you.

٥ . أذكروا نعمة الله عليكم .

6. O those who believe! Do not enter houses other than your own, until you have asked permission, and salute the inmates therein. That is best for you, that perhaps you may be heedful.

٦ . ياأيها الذين أمنوا لاتدخلوا بيوتا غير بيوتكم حتى تستأنسوا وتسلموا على أهلها ذلكم خير لكم لعلكم تذكرون .

7. Respect the guests and make their stay comfortable.

٧ . أكرموا الضيوف وأحسنوا مثواهم .

8. O Sabiha: clean the dining table, arrange the reception room and cook food for us.

٨ . يا صبيحة ! نظفى المائدة رتبى حجرة الجلوس واطبخى لنا الطعام .

9. Write your lesson, O Zainab.

٩ . اكتبى درسك يا زينب .

10. Do not go to your work late.

١٠ . لاتذهب إلى عملك متأخرا .

11. Feed the poor.

١١ . أطعم الفقراء .

12. Do not spy nor backbite each other.

١٢ . لاتجسسوا ولايغتب بعضكم بعضا .

13. Do not put off to-day's work for tomorrow.

١٣ . لا تؤخر عمل اليوم إلى غد

14. Walk on the road on the left side, stop if you see red light on the traffic signal. And help the blind and the weak in crossing the road.

١٤ . سِر فى الشارع على الطَّوار الأيسر قف إذا رأيت النور الاحمر فى إشارة المرور وساعد العمى والضعفاء على عُبور الشارع .

15. Listen to the advice of the doctor.

١٥ . إسمع نصيحة الطبيب .

16. O my brother! Do not leave the water tap open. Do not write on the wall of the house nor throw the waste paper and peel of the fruits except in the waste paper basket.

١٦ . ياأخى لاتترك صنبور الماء مفتوحا ولاتكتب على حائط البيت ولاترم الورق المهمل وقشر الفواكهِ إلا فى سلة المهملات .

17. Go to sleep early and wake up early.

١٧ . نم مبكرا واستيقظ مبكرا .

18. Respect the teacher.

١٨ . إحترم المعلم .

19. Memorise your lesson.

١٩ . إحفظ درسك .

20. Speak the truth.

٢٠ . إنطق بالصدق .

21. Do not laugh much.

٢١ . لاتكثر من الضحك .

22. Do not keep the company of the wicked.

٢٢ . لاتصاحب الأشرار .

23. Do not talk much, nor speak about what you do not know.

٢٣ . لاتكثر من الكلام ولاتنطق بما لاتعلم .

LESSON EIGHTEEN

ACTIVE AND PASSIVE VOICE المعروف والمجهول
TRANSITIVE AND INTRANSITIVE VERBS
الفعل المتعدى واللازم

Gardens of New Delhi.

حدائق دلهى الجديدة

1. Public gardens are developed in all parts of New Delhi. Green grass is grown in the ground. Trees are grown and benches are placed under the shadow of the trees.

١. تُنْشَأُ الْحَدَائِقُ الْعَامَّةُ فى جَميع أَنْحاءِ دلهى الجديدة وَيُزْرَعُ الحَشِيشُ الْأَخْضَرُ فى أَرْضِها وَتُغْرَسُ الْأَشْجارُ وَتوضَعُ المَقَاعِدُ فى ظِلِّ الشَّجَرِ.

2. The inhabitants of the city love these gardens. They enjoy the beautiful sights and inhale its pure air.

٢. وَسُكَّانُ الْمَدِينَةِ يُحِبُّونَ هذِه الحَدائِقَ وَيَتَمَتَّعُونَ بِمَنَاظِرِها الجَميلَةِ وَيَشُمُّونَ هَوَاءَها النَّقِيَّ.

3. It is seen that some boys pluck the flowers. That spoils the beauty of the garden.

٣. وَيُرَى أَنَّ بَعْضَ الاولاد يَقْتَطِفُونَ الازْهارَ. وَذلكَ يُفْسِدُ بَهْجَةَ الحَدِيقَةِ.

4. Do not touch the flowers of the public gardens nor walk on the grass.

٤. لاتَمُسْ يَدَكَ عَلى ازْهارِ الحَدائِقِ العامَّةِ وَلاتَمْشِى عَلى الحَشِيشِ.

ACTIVE AND PASSIVE VOICE   المعروف والمجهول

The verb in the active voice is called by the Arab Grammarians

الـفـعـل الـمـعـروف (المعـلوم) فاعـله *the action of which the agent is*

known. The verb in the passive voice is called الفعل المجهول فاعله
the action of which the agent is unknown.

PASSIVE مجهول	ACTIVE معروف
زُرِعَ القطنُ	زَرَعَ الفلاحُ القطنَ
Cotton was cultivated	*The peasant cultivated cotton*
كُسِرَ الزجاجةُ	قَدْ كَسَرَ الولدُ الزجاجةَ
The glass has been broken	*The boy has broken the glass*
يُصْنَعُ الكرسيُّ	يَصْنَعُ النَّجارُ الكرسيَّ
The chair is being made.	*The carpenter is making the chair.*

The sentences on the right, consist of a verb, a subject and an object. When compared with the sentences opposite to these, two major changes, in the construction of these sentences are found :

1. The verbs have been converted into the passive voice.

2. The subject of the active voice is an "agent", whose act affects an object. The subject of the passive voice is the object of sentences in the first group, it is called in Arabic نائب الفاعل

3. Further the verbs in the 2nd group are in concord with the gender of نائب الفاعل "Subject of the passive."

The passive is not used in Arabic when the agent of the act is expressed. A passive sentence in English such as : "A letter was written by Zaki" when rendered into Arabic would read كتب ذكى الرسالة *Zaki wrote the letter.*

The passive is formed from the active by a change of vowels.

In the past perfect, الماضى the first radical takes ُ the second radical takes ِ and the 3rd radical remains unchanged.

PASSIVE المجهول		ACTIVE المعروف	
he was beaten	ضُرِبَ	he beat	ضَرَبَ
he was heard	سُمِعَ	he heard	سَمِعَ
he was helped	نُصِرَ	he helped	نَصَرَ

In the Imperfect Tense, المضارع the prefix (sign of the Imperfect) takes ُ the 2nd radical takes َ and the last vowel is not disturbed.

PASSIVE المجهول		ACTIVE المعروف	
he is being beaten	يُضْرَبُ	he is beating	يَضْرِبُ
he is being heard	يُسْمَعُ	he is hearing	يَسْمَعُ
he is being helped	يُنْصَرُ	he is helping	يَنْصُرُ

TRANSITIVE AND INTRANSITIVE المتعدى واللازم

A discussion on the Active and Passive voice leads to the division of verbs into المتعدى the Transitive and اللازم the Intransitive.

A transitive verb, متعدى is a verb that denotes an action which passes over from the doer or subject to an object. In the sentence كَتَبَ التلميذُ مقالة The student wrote an essay, كتب is a transitive verb. Other examples of such verbs are :

زرع	ركب	كسر	ضرب	جر
to cultivate	to ride	to break	to strike	to pull

A verb, which expresses a state or condition or signifies an act which is confined to the subject, is an Intransitive verb, لازم . In the sentence جلس الولدُ على الكرسى *the boy sat on the chair,* جلس is an Intransitive verb. Some more examples of such verbs are:

ذهب	جاء	بكى	مرِض	نام
to go	*to come*	*to weep*	*to be sick*	*to sleep*

NOTE: Only transitive verbs can be used in the passive voice

The verbs on the pattern of كَرُمَ *to be generous,* are all Intransitive.

VOCABULARY

jawāz as-safar	جواز السفر	jamal	جمل
passport		*camel*	
tashira	تأشيرة	süf	صوف
visa		*wool*	
hajz	حجز	qutn	قطن
reservation		*cotton*	
mutamassik	متمسك	harir	حرير
holding		*silk*	
zāra	زار ـ يزور	tabarra'	تبرع
to visit		*to contribute, donate*	
zāir	زائر	bursa	برصة
visitor		*stock exchange*	
ziyara	زيارة	yatim	يتيم ـ يتامى
visit		*orphan*	
kashāb	خشب	armala	أرملة
wood, timbėr		*widow*	
qatala	قتل ـ يقتل	daman	ضمان
to kill		*surety, guaranty*	
jabhat ulqitāl	جبهة القتال	ta'min	تأمين
war front		*insurance*	

ishtirakiya	إشتراكية	taura	ثورة : هياج
socialism		rising, rebellion	
räsmäliya	رأسمالية	tamattaa	تمتع : إستمتع
capitalism		to enjoy	
hatab	حطب	shamma	شم : إشتم
fire-wood		to smell	
ansha'	أنشأ	nazif	نظيف : نقى
establish		pure, clean	
äsif	آسف	raunaq	رونق : بهجة
sorry, sad		splendour	
hukümah	حكومة	särüq	صاروخ
government, rule		rocket	
'ämm	عام ـ شامل	banä	بنى : إبتنى
general, public		to build	
al aman al-ämm	الامن العام	binäya	بناية
public security		building	
arräi al-ämm	الرأى العام	qabada	قبض ـ يقبض
public opinion		to hold, arrest	
nazama	نظم : إنتظم	qabd	قبض : مسك
to organise, arrange		constipation, grasping	
nizäm	نظام : ترتيب	qabr	قبر
arrangement,system		grave	
'inab	عنب	maqbüd	مقبوض
grapes		occupied, possessed	
surür	سرور : مسرة : فرح	qänün	قانون
delight		law, code	
musäbaqa	مسابقة الخطابية	qämüs	قاموس ـ قواميس
oratorical contest		dictionary	
tära	ثار : هاج	aalana	أعلن ـ يعلن
to rise, rebel		to declare, announce	

al imtihän *annual examination*	الامتحان السنوية	zill *shadow, shade*	ظل
gubär *dust*	غبار : تراب	qita' *part, piece*	قطعة
garasa *to plant trees*	غرس ـ يغرس	nazzafa *to clean*	نظف
asliha *weapon, arms*	أسلحة	massa *to touch*	مس ـ يمس

Observe the use of the verb in the passive voice, in the following sentences :

TRANSLATION	MODEL SENTENCES
1. Clothes are woven from wool, or cotton or silk.	١ . تُنسج الثياب من الصوف أو القطن أو الحرير .
2. Donation is collected for the aid of the poor, the disabled and the orphans.	٢ . تُجمع التبرعات لمساعدة الفقراء والمساكين واليتامى .
3. Leather was exported to foreign countries.	٣ . صُدرت الجلود إلى الخارج .
4. Prizes have been distributed to the winners of the match.	٤ . قد قُسمت الجوائز للفائزين فى المبارات .
5. The rocket has been fired.	٥ . قد أُطلق الصاروخ .
6. The house was constructed with speed.	٦ . شُيّد البناء بسرعة .
7. The parrot was caged.	٧ . قُفص البغاء .
8. Money has been stolen.	٨ . قد سُرق المال .
9 The results of the annual examination were announced.	٩ . أُعلن نتائج الامتحانات السنوية .

10. Rabindranath Tagore was born in Calcutta and he was teaching in Shantiniketan.

١٠ . وُلد رابندرنات طاغور فى كلكتا وكان يُدرّس فى شانتى نكيتن .

11. The child slept in the cradle.

١١ . نام الطفل فى المهد .

12. The visitor sat on the chair.

١٢ . جلس الزائر على الكرسى .

13. The student went out of his house.

١٣ . خرج التلميذ من بيته .

14. The girl became happy with the reward.

١٤ . فرحت البنت بالجائزة .

15. The chair is made of wood.

١٥ . يُصنع الكرسى بالخشب .

16. The soldier has been killed on the war front.

١٦ . قد قُتل الجندى على جبهة القتال .

17. The camel carried the fire-wood.

١٧ . حَمل الجمل الحطب .

18. The firewood has been carried.

١٨ . قد حُمل الحطب .

19. The Government develops public gardens.

١٩ . تَنشأ الحكومة الحدائق العامة .

20. Public gardens are being developed.

٢٠ . تُنشأ الحدائق العامة .

21. The gardener is planting the tree.

٢١ . يَغرس البستانى الشجر .

22. The tree is being planted.

٢٢ . يُغرس الشجر .

23. The engineer lays the streets.

٢٣ . يُنَظِّم المهندس الطرق .

24. The streets are being laid.

٢٤ . تُنظَّم الطرق .

25. Grapes have been cultivated in the garden of the school.

٢٥ . زُرعت العنب فى حديقة المدرسة .

26. I was happy at the success of my friend in the oratorical contest.

٢٦ . سُررتُ بنجاح صديقى فى مسابقة الخطابة .

27. The dust rose.

٢٧ . ثار الغبار .

28. The wind blew.

٢٨ . هبَّت الريح .

MOODS OF THE IMPERFECT TENSE

المضارع المنصوب والمضارع المجزوم

INDUSTRIAL CENTRE	مركز الصناعة

١. أَرادَ راجَن أَن يَزُور المركزَ الصِّناعِيَّ فى "جندى" فَعَرَضَ هذه الفِكْرَةَ عَلى والِده وطَلَبَ مِنهُ أَنْ يَصْحَبَهُ إلى "جندى"

1. Rajan wanted to visit the Industrial estate at Guindy and he placed this idea before his father. He requested his father to accompany him to Guindy.

٢. فَقَال الوالد : لِماذَا تُحِبُّ أَنْ تَزُورَ تِلكَ المِنْطَقَةَ .

2. The father asked : "Why do you wish to visit that area?

٣. قال راجن : أُحِبُّ أَنْ أُشاهِدَ ما فِيها مِن مَصْنُوعات كَثيرَةٍ كَىْ تَنْمُوَ مَعْلُوماتِى ولأَعْرِفَ صُورَةً واضِحَةً عَنْ نَشاطِنا فى مَيْدَانِ الصِّناعَةِ .

3. Rajan replied : "I wish to see many of the things manufactured there so that my knowledge increases and to have a clear picture of our progress in the Industrial field."

٤. سُرَّ الوالد مِن إجابةِ راجن وقال لَهُ : سَأُصاحِبُكَ يا راجن وَلَكِن عَلَيكَ أَن تَكْتُبَ عَن كُلّ ما يُعجِبُكَ .

4. The father was happy with Rajan's reply and he told him : "I will accompany you Rajan, but it is necessary that you write down what appeals to you."

INTRODUCTION

The Imperfect Tense, الفعل المضارع, conveys the meaning of the present and the future tense. But due to the addition of certain particles before it, the meaning of مضارع undergoes a change, and sometimes change occurs not only in the meaning but also in the word. As mentioned earlier, the addition of سوف and س before مضارع converts it into the future tense.

CHANGES IN THE MEANING OF IMPERFECT

The Imperfect المضارع has five moods, which are distinguished by the vowel of the third radical. In this respect it resembles the Noun الاسم with its three case-endings.

The simplest use of a verb is to make a statement of fact, or ask a question. But a verb may also be used to express a command; or to express a mere supposition or a wish. These different manners in which a verb may be used to express an action are called moods.

The Imperfect المضارع has five moods; namely, the Indicative, Subjunctive, Jussive or conditional, Imperative and Energetic.

The Indicative and the Imperative have been dealt with in lessons 16 and 17 respectively.

PARTICLES WHICH CHANGE THE MEANING OF THE IMPERFECT

There are three groups of particles which place either ــَ , or ــْ or the ن of emphasis at the end of the Imperfect. With this addition it is called (1) المضارع المنصوب *the subjunctive* (2) المضارع المجزوم *the Jussive* and المضارع مع نـون التاكيد *the Energetic of the Imperfect*, respectively. But in the absence of any of these particles الفعل المضارع *the Imperfect* will end with "Dammah" ــُ

THE SUBJUNCTIVE   المضارع المنصوب

The particles which give ﹷ to the مضارع are:

(1) أَنْ *that*   (2) لَنْ *certainly not*   (3) إذَنْ *in that case*

(4) كَى *in order that*

e.g. 1. أَنْ يَذْهَبَ   2. لَنْ يَذْهَبَ   3. إذَنْ يَذْهَبَ   4. كَى يَذْهَبَ

That he goes   *He will never*   *in that case*   *in order that*
           go   *he goes*   *he goes*

THE JUSSIVE   المضارع المجزوم

The particles which give ﹿ to the مضارع are :- (1) لَمْ *Not* (2) لام الامر *The* ل *of command*, (3) لا النهى *the* لا *of prohibition.* (It expresses a prohibition or a wish that something is not to be done) (4) إنْ *if* and (5) لَمَّا *never.*

e.g. (1) لَمْ يَفْعَلْ   (2) لِيُنْفِقْ ذو سَعَةٍ   (3) لا تَحْزَنْ

He did not do   *The prosperous*   *Do not grieve*
              shall spend

(4) إنْ تَعْجَلْ تَنْدَمْ   (5) لَمَّا يَضْرِبْ

If you make haste   *He never beat*
you will repent

THE ENERGETIC OF THE IMPERFECT   المضارع مع نون التأكيد

"The ن of emphasis" comes at the end of مضارع after ل "lam with fathah" is prefixed to it.

لَيَفْعَلَنَّ *he will certainly do.* لَيَنْصُرَنَّ الله *certainly God will help.*

The "Energetic" forms of the Imperfect المضارع have always a future sense. e.g.

لَئِنْ أُنْجَيْتَنا مِنْ هذه لَنَكُونَنَّ مِنَ الشَّاكِرِينَ *If you deliver us from this (danger), certainly we will be from the thankful.*

VOCABULARY

kibr *old age*	كبر	mizäniya *balance, budget*	ميزانية
sigar *young age*	صغر	aräda *to wish, to desire*	أراد ـ يريد
min fadlak *please*	من فضلك	iräda *will, choice*	'دة : مشية
mustarih *relaxing, comfortable*	مستريح	ahabba *to love*	أحب ـ يحب
rajä' *hope, request*	رجاء	waqafa *to stand*	وقف ـ يقف
tämim *nationalisation*	تأميم	auqafa *to prevent, to stop*	أوقف : منع
amäna *reliability, trust*	أمانة	mauqaf *attitude, position*	موقف
sarafa *to spend, to change money*	صرف ـ يصرف	waqf *endowment*	وقف ـ أوقاف
masrif *bank*	مصرف : بنك	shurti *policeman*	شرطى : بوليس
haqq *legal claim, truth*	حق ـ حقوق	harkat al murür *the traffic*	حركة المرور
ista'dda *to get ready, prepare*	إستعد	tafaddal *please yourself*	تفضل
musta'id *prepared, ready*	مستعد	kahrabä' *electricity*	كهرباء
musä'ida *aid, help*	مساعدة	taktit *planning*	تخطيط
battäl *unemployed*	بطال	dagata *to press*	ضغط
wazifa *job, employment*	وظيفة : خدمة	alqä *to throw*	ألقى ـ يلقى

alqä bayanan an ألقى بيانا عن
to make a statement about

ittihäd إتحاد : وفاق
unity, union

jam'iya taäwuniyya جمعية تعاونية
co-operative society

niqäba نقابة
trade union, guild

kaslän كسلان
lazy

raqäba رقابة
censorship

tat'im تطعيم
vaccination

daula دولة
state, country

badla بدلة
suit

mustadim مستديم
constant

qaddama قدم ـ يقدم
to offer, to present

kallama كلم ـ يكلم
to speak

sinn سن ـ أسنان
tooth, age, tip

haflatu ashshai حفلة الشاى
tea party

mi'taf معطف
overcoat

masjid مسجد
mosque

räfaqa رافق
to accompany

sitär ستار
curtain, veil

ihtamma إهتم ـ يهتم
to pay attention

mintaqa منطقة
zone, area

saräha صراحة
frankness

huküma حكومة
government

mindil منديل
kerchief

nashara نشر ـ ينشر
to spread, unfold

juräb جراب
sock

kibrit كبريت
matches, sulfur

adda أدى
to discharge, carry out

dukän دخان
smoke

alumam almuttahida الامم المتحدة
The United Nations

'asal عسل
honey

shahr al'asal *honeymoon*	شهر العسل	maidän *field, square*	ميدان
mustawal hayä *standard of living*	مستوى الحياة	mallah *sailor, mariner*	ملاح
shaqqa *flat, apartment*	شقة	duwali *international*	دولى
shabi'a *to be satisfied*	شبع ـ يشبع	täbaq *storey, floor*	طابق
shab'än *satisfied, full*	شبعان	fikra *thought, idea*	فكرة
ma'lümät *information, data*	معلومات	hädita *accident, event*	حادثة
istilämät *inquiry office*	إستعلامات	süra *picture, photo*	صورة
a'jiba *to astonish, to admire*	أعجب	sahaba *to withdraw, pull out*	سحب ـ يسحب

Observe the use of the Imperfect tense in different forms, in the following sentences.

TRANSLATION	MODEL SENTENCES
1. I wish to visit Arab countries.	١ . أريد أن أزور البلدان العربية
2. I like to play foot-ball.	٢ . أحب أن ألعب كرة القدم .
3. The policeman stood to regulate traffic.	٣ . وقف الشرطى كى ينظم المرور .
4. I purchased a ticket that I may watch the Hockey match.	٤ . إشتريت تذكرة كى أشاهد مباراة «هاكى» .
5. Man toils in his young age that he could relax in old age.	٥ . يتعب المرأ فى صغره كى يستريح فى كبره .

6. Mrs. Indira Gandhi has nationalised the banks to restore the right to the sons of the soil.

٦ . أممت السيدة إندرا غاندى البنوك ليرجع الحق إلى أبناء الوطن .

7. The student prepared to deliver a speech in the meeting (gathering).

٧ . إستعد التلميذ ليلقى كلمة فى الحفلة .

8. The officer will never delay his work.

٨ . لن يتأخر الموظف عن عمله .

9. The lazy person never succeeds.

٩ . لن يفوز الكسلان .

10. Work with sincerity that you may receive great reward from God.

١٠ . إعمل باخلاص حتى تنال الجزاء العظيم من الله .

11. It pleases me to offer my thanks to all those who have attended the function.

١١ . يسرنى أن أقدم شكرى لكل من إشترك فى الحفلة .

12. The father instructed his son to wash his teeth before and after sleep.

١٢ . أمر الوالد إبنه أن يغسل أسنانه قبل النوم وبعدها .

13. Be polite, so that you could be acceptable.

١٣ . كن مؤدَّبا كى تكونَ محبوبا .

14. I went to Basrah in order to learn the Arabic language.

١٤ . ذهبتُ إلى البصرة كى أتعلم اللغة العربية .

15. I acquire knowledge in order to serve my country and my people.

١٥ . أتعلم كى أخدم وطنى وأهلى .

16. The State pays attention to the development of industry so that the standard of living may rise.

١٦ . تهتم الدولة بنشر الصناعة ليرقى مستوى المعيشة .

17. The sailor raises the sail of the boat so that the wind may push it.

١٧ . ينشر الملّاح شراع السفينة ليدفعها الهواء .

18. I never eat whilst I am satisfied, (saturated).

١٨ . لن آكل وأنا شبعان .

19. The peasant never sells his land.

١٩ . لن يبيع الفلاح أرضه .

20. The student said to his teacher, "I have completed my home work." The teacher replied to him, "in that case you will succeed."

٢٠ . قال التلميذ لاستاذه : لقد أديت واجبى فأجاب الاستاذ : إذن تنجح .

21. The attendant did not come yesterday.

٢١ . لم يحضر الفرّاش البارحة .

22. Do not grieve ; certainly God is with you.

٢٢ . لا تحزن إن الله معك .

LESSON TWENTY

كان وأخواتها AND ITS SISTERS **كان**

فيصل

FAISAL

1. Faisal is a sportsman. He learnt swimming and became strong in mind and body.

فَيْصَل شاب رِياضِيٌّ تَعَلَّمَ السِّباحَةَ فَقَد صَارَ فيصل قَوِيًّا صَحيحَ الْجِسْمِ والْعَقْلِ .

2. One day Faisal woke up early in the morning. He was walking on the bank of a river which was near his village. He was extremely happy as the weather was clear and the sun was not warm.

وفى يَوْمٍ مِنَ الأَيَّامِ أَصْبَحَ فَيْصَل مُبَكِّرا وكان يَمْشى على شاطِئِ نَهْرٍ الْقَرِيبَةِ مِنْ قَرْيَتِهِ وكان فى غايَةِ السُّرُورِ إذ أَضحى الجَوُّ صَحواً ولَيسَتِ الشَّمْسُ مُحْرِقَةً .

3. As Faisal walked on the river bank, he saw a boy about to be drowned in the river. He rushed towards him. He rescued him and rendered him first-aid. He removed water from his abdomen and remained by his side till the boy recovered consciousness. He advised him : "Do not get into the river so long as the current is strong,"

وظَلَّ فيصل سائراً على شاطِئِ إذ رَأى صَبِيًّا يَكادُ يَغْرِقُ فى النَّهرِ فَهرَوَلَ إِلَيهِ وأَنْقَذَهُ وأَسْعَفَهُ وأَخْرَجَ الماء مِنْ بَطْنِهِ ومازالَ فيصل على جانِبِهِ حَتى أفاقَ الصَّبِىُّ مِن إغْماء وقالَ له لاتَنْزِل النَّهْرَ مادامَ التَّيَّارُ شَديدا .

4. Then he took him to his house. The family was shocked when it learnt about the accident, and thanked Faisal for his timely help.The mother spent the night delighted at the safety of her beloved son. And the family spent the night thanking God for His favour and mercy.

٤ . ثُمَّ أَخَذَهُ إلى بَيْتِهِ ودَهِشَتِ الأُسْرَةُ عِنْدَما عَلِمَتْ بِالحادِثِ وشَكَرَتْ فَيْصَل لِمُساعَدَتِهِ . فأمْسَتِ الأُمُّ قَرِيرَةَ العَيْن بِنَجاةِ وَلَدِها الحَبِيبِ وباتَتِ الأُسْرَةُ شاكِرَةً لِفَضْلِ اللهِ ورَحْمَتِهِ ونِعَمِهِ .

There are certain verbs and particles which, when introduced at the beginning of a nominal sentence, bring about certain vowel changes in respect of their subject and predicate. Verbs of Incomplete predication i.e. كان and its sisters الأفعال الناقصة are discussed in this lesson.

The Verbs of Incomplete Predication *الأفعال الناقصة express the idea of becoming or a state of continuation. When it is said كان أحمد *Ahmed was*, the person who hears this expression might as well ask : "What was Ahmed?" But, when it is stated كان أحمد تاجرا *Ahmed was a merchant*, the predicate is complete. This nominal sentence is analysed thus :

The verb of incomplete predication	كان ـ الفعل الناقص
The subject of Käna	أحمد ـ إسم كان
The predicate of Käna	تاجرا ـ خبر كان

According to the rules governing the subject and predicate in a nominal sentence, the vowels of the last letter of the two should be the same, (vide lesson No. 9). But when كان and the verbs which fall under this category are introduced at the beginning of a nominal sentence ;

---

*Literal meaning : *the incomplete Verbs.*

1. the subject of **كان** will be in the nominative case : **مرفوع ــُ**

2. the predicate of **كان** will be in the accusative case : **منصوب ــَ**

The list of **الافعال الناقصة** or **كان** and its·sisters is given below :

1. to be	كانَ	8. not to be	لَيْسَ
2. to become	صارَ	9. to continue	ما زالَ
3. to become at dawn	أصْبَحَ	10. to continue	ما بَرِحَ
4. to become in the forenoon	أضْحَى	11. to continue	ما فتِىَ
5. to become in the evening	أمْسى	12. to continue	مَاانَفَكَّ
6. to become during night	باتَ	13. as long as	مادام
7. to remain	ظَلَّ		

All the verbs belonging to the category of **كان** are converted to past and Imperfect tenses and are conjugated likewise.

In the following chart, the nominal sentences are written without and with **كان** and its sisters. Note the vowel changes that occur as a result of the insertion of **كان** or verbs belonging to its group.

The boy was playing.	كان الولدُ لاعباً	كان	الولدُ لاعبُ
The wheather became hot.	صار الجوُّ حارا	صار	الجوُّ حارُّ
Rain became abudant at dawn.	أصبح المطرُ غزيرا	أصبح	المطرُ غزيرُ
The traveller became tired (at noon)	أضحى المسافر متعبا	أضحى	المسافرُ متعبُ
The girl became happy (in the evening).	أمست البنت مسرورةً	أمسى	البنت مسرورةُ

The patient slept during the night.	بات المريضُ نائما بات	المريضُ نائمٌ
The soldier remained brave.	ظلَّ الجنديُّ شجاعا ظلَّ	الجنديُّ شجاعٌ
The building is not strong.	ليس البناءُ قوياً ليس	البناءُ قويٌ
Hatim continues to be rich.	مازال حاتم غنياً مازال	حاتم غنى
The worker continues to be hard-working.	مافتئ العاملُ مجتهداً مافتئ	العاملُ مجتهدٌ
The merchant continues to be trustworthy.	ماانفك التاجر صادقاً ماانفك	التاجرُ صادقٌ

CONJUGATION OF كان *TO BE*

Future & Present tense		المضارع		Past tense		الماضى
Plural	Dual	Sing.	Plural	Dual	Sing.	
يَكونونَ	يَكونانِ	يَكونُ	كانُوا	كانا	كانَ	3rd Per. Mas.
يَكُنَّ	تكونانِ	تكونُ	كُنَّ	كائتا	كانتْ	3rd Per. Fem.
تكزنونَ	تكونانِ	تكونُ	كنتُم	كنتما	كُنْتَ	2nd Per. Mas.
تَكُنَّ	تكونانِ	تكونين	كنتُنَّ	كنتما	كُنتِ	2nd Per. Fem.
نكونُ	نكونُ	أكونُ	كُنَّا	كُنَّا	كُنْتُ	First Per. Mas./Fem.

he will be   يكونُ   he was   كانَ

you do not be   لا تَكُنْ   you be   كُنْ

كان is also used to form "past continuous" and "distant past"

he was going/he used to go (Past continuous)   كان يذهب   he had gone (Distant past)   كان ذهب

VOCABULARY

gariqa	غرق ـ يغرق	mutarjim	مترجم
to sink, plunge		translator	
istagraqa	إستغرق ـ يستغرق	jamada	جمد
to engage, absorb		to harden, to freeze	
harwala	هرول ـ يهرول	'ämil	عامل ـ عمال
to hasten, walk fast		a worker, doer	
anqada	أنقذ ـ ينقذ	riyadi	رياضى
to rescue, save		sportsman, mathematician	
munäqasha	مناقشة	riyäda	رياضة : تمرين
discussion		exercise, practice	
is'äf	إسعاف	sahih	صحيح
relief, first aid		correct, healthy, right	
akraja	أخرج	kanisa	كنيسة
to send out, bring out		synagogue, temple, church	
mutakarrij	متخرج	mauqid	موقد
graduate		stove	
musajjil	مسجل	gäya	غاية : غرض
registrar, tape recorder		goal, aim, intent	
halläq	حلاق	furn	فرن
barber		oven	
kayät	خياط	haraqa	حرق ـ يحرق
tailor		to burn	
musawwir	مصور	harräqa	حراقة
photographer		torpedo boat	
hai'a	هيئة	hariq	حريق : حريقة
shape, organisation		fire, conflagration	

tayyär تيار : مجرى
current, tide, course

fursa dahabiya فرصة ذهبية
golden opportunity

tayyär mubäshir تيار مباشر
direct current

mashwara مشورة
consultation, advice

tayyär mutanawib تيار متناوب
alternating current

täba yawmakum طاب يومكم
good day

mudhish مدهش
amazing, marvelous

hazzan sayidan حظا سعيدا
good luck

qurrat al'ain قرة العين
darling, delight of the eye

fi aman Allah فى أمان الله
in the protection of God

wa'ada وعد
to promise

jämiat al - Azhar جامعة الازهر
Al-Azhar University

mau'id موعد
appointed time, pledge

muttaham متهم
accused, defendant

didd ضد
a contrary, opponent

muttahim متهم
accuser, prosecutor

shajrat närjil شجرة نارجيل
coconut tree

ittahama إتهم
to accuse

misbah مصباح
lamp

bari' برئ
guiltless, free from

rumman رمان
pomegranate

mu'tamar مؤتمر
conference, congress

mana'a منع - يمنع
to prevent, hinder

mustamir مستمر
continuous, lasting

mamnü' ممنوع
prohibited, banned

qanäh قناة : ترعة
canal, tube

wahm وهم
suspicion, doubt

faidän فيضان
flood

nizä' نزاع
dispute, struggle

hadaf هدف
target, objective

'äsifa عاصفة
storm, tempest

muwäsala مواصلة
communication

shäwara شاور : إستشار
to consult

irtifä إرتفاع
increase, height

sabäh al-kair صباح الخير
good morning

sawäsiya سواسية
equal, alike

masä' al-lair مساء الخير
good evening

furshat asnaän فرشة أسنان،
tooth brush

ila al-liqä' إلى اللقاء
let us meet again

fadl فضل : إحسان
favour, kindness

jämid جامد
hard, solid, frozen

mustahil مستحيل
impossible

imära إمارة ـ إمارات
emirate

färig فارغ
empty, un-occupied

dabala ذبل
to wither, fade

infijär إنفجار
explosion, outbreak

däbil ذابل
withering, dried up

dakara ذخر : إذخر
to store, to keep

shätir شاطر
cunning, smart

dakira ذخيرة
treasure, supplies

farra فر ـ يفر
to escape, flee

marhun مرهون
mortgaged

muzdahim مزدحم
crowded

zahama زحم
to crowd

miftäh مفتاح
key

qufl قفل
lock

zukrug زخرف
decoration

asir أسير
prisoner of war

takfid تخفيض
discount, reduction

fadiha فضيحة
disgraceful

mustashriq مستشرق
orientalist

wasiya وصية
will, testament

Make a note of the use of **كان** and allied verbs in the following sentences :

TRANSLATION	MODEL SENTENCES
1. The garden was open.	١ . كانت الحديقة مفتوحة .
2. The wind became cold.	٢ . صار الهواء باردا .
3. Zaki is not sick.	٣ . ليس ذكى مريضا .
4. Lakshmi is not lazy.	٤ . ليست لكشمى كسلانة .
5. Water became frozen (at dawn).	٥ . أصبح الماء جامدا .
6. The day became hot (in the forenoon).	٦ . أضحى اليوم حارا .
7. The flower became withered (in the evening).	٧ . أمسى الزهر ذابلا .
8. The dog remained watchful.	٨ . ظل الكلب حارسا .
9. The watchman was standing (during night).	٩ . بات الحارس قائما .
10. Hamid is still in Iraq.	١٠ . لا يزال حامد فى العراق .
11. He has enjoined upon me prayer and alms-giving, so long as I remain alive.	١١ . أوصانى بالصلوة والزكواة ما دمت حيا .
12. The wind continues to be violent.	١٢ . مافتى الريح شديدا .
13. The market continues to be crowded.	١٣ . ماانفك السوق مزدحمة .
14. The aeroplane was about to explode.	١٤ . كادت الطائرة تنفجر .

15. Success is not easy.

١٥ . لا نجاح سهلا .

16. The army started moving.

١٦ . شرع الجيش يتحرك .

17. Friendship is not permanent without sincerity.

١٧ . لا صداقة دائمة بغير إخلاص

18. The student (f) started preparing for the examination.

١٨ . أخذت التلميذة تستعد للامتحان .

19. India became a great nation after independence.

١٩ . أصبحت الهند دولة كبرى بعد الاستقلال .

20. The weather became pleasant in spring.

٢٠ . صار الجو لطيفا فى الربيع .

21. The playground is not crowded with people.

٢١ . ليس ميدان اللعب مزدحما من الناس .

22. The people remain marching on the way to progress.

٢٢ . سيظل الشعب سائرا فى طريق الرقى والتقدم .

23. The patient is still in the hospital.

٢٣ . مازال المريض فى المستشفى .

24. The train was slow near the station.

٢٤ . كان القطار بطيئا قرب المحطة .

25. The peasant became happy with the fruit of his labour.

٢٥ . أصبح الفلاح سعيدا بثمر جهوده .

26. The worker became tired in the evening.

٢٦ . أمسى العامل متعبا .

27. The lamp was burning in the night.

٢٧ . بات المصباح متقدا .

28. You will not succeed so long as you are lazy.

٢٨ . لا تنجح مادمتَ كسلانا .

LESSON TWENTYONE

إن وأخواتها AND ITS SISTERS إن

THE BANKS	المصارف «البنوك»

1. Banks are very essential in every country.

١. إنَّ المَصارِفَ ضَرُورِيةٌ فى كلِّ بَلَدٍ.

2. Because they (banks) keep (in safe custody) money and benefit the merchants and others and undertake conversion of money in different currencies.

٢. لأنَّها تَحْفَظُ الأمْوالَ وتُفيدُ التُّجَّارَ وَغَيْرَهُمْ وتَقُومُ بِتَحْويلِ النُّقُودِ إلى عُمْلات مُخْتَلِفَةٍ.

3. Would that the highly rich acknowledge its use (objective; message)!

٣. ولَيْتَ كِبارَ الأغْنِياءِ يَعْتَرِفُونَ بِرِسالَتِها.

4. But some of them are afraid of government interference in its affairs (conduct).

٤. لكِنَّ بَعْضَهُمْ خَائِفٌ مِنْ تَدَخُّلِ الحُكُومَةِ فى مُعامَلاتِها.

5. And perhaps the Government will supervise over them (banks) completely (complete supervision) in the interest of the people.

٥. ولَعَلَّ الدَّولةَ مُشْرِفَةٌ عَلَيها إشْرافا كامِلا لِمَصْلَحَةِ الشَّعَب.

6. (And) the employees of the banks are a cultured people as if every one (individual) among them is an angel from the sky.

٦. ومُوظِّفُوا المصارِفِ قَومٌ مُهَذَّبُونَ وكأنَّ كلَّ فَرْدٍ مِنْهُم ملك مِنَ السَّماءِ.

7. It is necessary on (the part of) every individual to deposit (keep) a part of his income in the bank so much so we can build our country and that it would (the deposit) be helpful to us at the (time of) need.

٧ . فَعَلى كُلِّ فَرِدٍ أَنْ يَدَّخِرَ جُزْءًا مِنْ دَخْلِهِ فِى البنك حَتى نَبْنِى بَلَدَنا وَيكونُ عَوْناً لنا عِنْدَ الحاجَةِ .

When إن and its sisters are added to a nominal sentence, the meaning of the sentence changes and also the vowel of their subject and predicate الهَرَمُ قَدِيمٌ means, *the pyramid is old,* but with the addition of إن as in إنَّ الهَرَمَ قَدِيمٌ the sentence would mean *certainly the pyramid is old.* This sentence is analysed thus :

إنَّ	*certainly*	الحروف المشبه بالفعل	The particle which resembles the verb	
الهرم	*Pyramid*	إسم إنَّ	The subject of	إنَّ
قديم	*old*	خبر إنَّ	The predicate of	إنَّ

These particles bring about a vowel change in their subject and predicate exactly in the opposite fashion as كان i.e.

1. The subject of إنَّ will be in the accusative case, منصوب -َ

2. The predicate of إنَّ will be in the nominative case, مرفوع -ُ

The particles which are called إنَّ and its sisters are as follows, and all these have been used in the illustrative text above (Page :131)

perhaps	لَعَلَّ (٥)	as if	كأنَّ (٣)	certainly	إنَّ (١)
would that	لَيْتَ (٦)	but	لكنَّ (٤)	that	أنَّ (٢)

COMMERCIAL VOCABULARY

qüwat as-shirä *purchasing power*	قوة الشراء	rusüm jumrukia *customs duties*	رسوم جمركية
mablag *a sum, amount*	مبلغ	indat talab *on demand*	عند الطلب
al majmu' *the total*	المجموع	matlüb *wanted, due*	مطلوب
taman *price, cost, value*	ثمن ـ اثمان	dain *debt, liability*	دين ـ ديون
qima *value, worth*	قيمة	shirä' *purchase*	شراء
irtifä al as'är *price rise*	إرتفاع الاسعار	bai' *sale*	بيع
takfid al as'är *price reduction*	تخفيض الاسعار	bai bil jumla *whole sale*	بيع بالجملة
säfi al humüla *net tonnage*	صافى الحمولة	bai bil mufrad *retail*	بيع بالمفرد
mizäniya *balance sheet, budget*	ميزانية	al-bai naqdan *sale on cash*	البيع نقدا
tasfiya *liquidation*	تصفية	al-bai dainan *sale on credit*	البيع دينا
sharik *partner*	شريك ـ شركاء	sharika *company, corporation*	شركة
ishtiräk *partnership, subscription*	إشتراك	'ayyina *sample, specimen*	عينة
taqsit *payment in instalments*	تقسيط	namüdaj *pattern, model*	نموذج
musähim *share-holder*	مساهم	sahm *share*	سهم
mu'assasa *establishment : company*	مؤسسة : شركة	rusüm ash shahn *the freight*	رسوم الشحن

dafa'
دفعة
payment, thrust

dafätir
دفاتر ـ سجلات
journals, ledgers

bülsat ash shahn
بولسة الشحن
bill of lading

maktab
مكتب
office, bureau

'aläma musajjala
علامة مسجلة
trade - mark

kätib
كاتب
clerk, typist

hisäb
حساب
accounting, calculation

sarräf
صراف
cashier, money changer

hisäb jarin
حساب جار
current account

musäid
مساعد
assistant

hisäb al taufir
حساب التوفير
saving account

wakil
وكيل
agent, attorney

hasm
حسم
discounting, settling

wakäla
وكالة
agency, power of attorney

ijrä't qänüniya
إجراءات قانونية
legal steps

bidä'a
بضاعة ـ بضائع
goods

taflisa
تفليسة
bankruptcy

fätüra
فاتورة
invoice, bill

ta'rid al kasära
تعريض الخسارة
indemnity

wasl
وصل ـ ايصال
voucher, receipt

ribh
ربح
interest, benefit

umla sa'ba
عملة صعبة
hard currency

fäida
فائدة
profit, use

umla sahla
عملة سهلة
soft currency

kasära
خسارة
loss, damage

naqd
نقد
money, cash

dakl
دخل
income, receipts

fakka
فكة ـ صرافة
small coins

räs mäl
رأس مال
capital

gineh
جنيه
pound (English or Egyptian)

'aläma *mark, emblem*	علامة : مارك	'ard *offer, display, supply*	عرض
dinär *Dinar (Iraqi, Kuwaiti)*	دينار	talabiya *order*	طلبية
dirham *Dirham (U.A.E)*	درهم	tämin *insurance*	تأمين
fils *small coins*	فلس ـ فلوس	amin *honest, reliable*	أمين
riyäl *Saudi currency*	ريال	tasdir *export, sending*	تصدير
dolär *Dollar*	دولار	taurid *import*	توريد
tijära *commerce*	تجارة	älat al kitäba *typewriter*	آلة الكتابة
kambiyäla *bill of exchange, draft*	كمبيالة	mu'ämala *transaction, conduct*	معاملة
hawäla *promissory note*	حوالة	tadakkul *interference, intervention*	تدخل
mazäd *auction*	مزاد	muwazzaf *official, employee*	موظف
munäqasa *tender*	مناقصة	shart *condition*	شرط
muwäfaqa *approval, sanction*	موافقة	'aqd *contract, agreement*	عقد : معاهدة
rahn *mortgage*	رهن	qard *loan*	قرض
'umüla *commission, brokerage*	عمولة	tahwil *conversion, transfer*	تحويل
ilqa' *cancellation, termination*	الغاء : انهاء	talab *demand, claim*	طلب

simsär	سمسار	i'tiräf	اعتراف
broker, middleman		*recognition*	
dariba	ضريبة ـ ضرائب	daleel	دليل
tax, duty		*directory, evidence*	
daribat ad-dakl	ضريبة الدخل	watiqa	وثيقة
income tax		*document, record*	
daribat kasb	ضريبة كسب العمل	darüra	ضرورة : حاجة
wage tax		*need, want*	
'ämil	عامل ـ عمال	risäla	رسالة
workman, labour		*letter, message*	

Make a note of the use of إن and allied particles in the following sentences :

TRANSLATION	*MODEL SENTENCES*
1. Certainly God is with the steadfast.	١ . إن الله مع الصابرين
2. As if the news were correct.	٢ . كأنَّ الخبر صحيح .
3. The plane fell but the loss is small.	٣ . سقطت الطيارة لكن الخسارة قليلة .
4. Would that the accused is free.	٤ . ليت المتهم برئ .
5. Perhaps the conference is continuing.	٥ . لعل المؤتمر مستمر .
6. I know that fish is abundant in this pond.	٦ . أنا أعرف أن السمك كثير فى هذه الترعة .
7. The water during the moonlit night was as if it was silver that shines.	٧ . كأنَّ الماء فضة لامعة فى ليلة مقمرة .

8. Certainly Bombay is the biggest port in India.

٨ . إنَّ بومباى أكبر ميناء فى الهند .

9. Would that, world peace is permanent.

٩ . لَيتَ السلام العالمى دائم .

10. Perhaps the train is reaching the station as per schedule.

١٠ . لعلَّ القطار يصل المحطة فى موعده .

11. The tree is big but it is without fruit.

١١ . الشجرة كبيرة لكنها غير مثمرة .

12. We have no knowledge except that which You (God) had taught us.

١٢ . لا علم لنا الا ما علمتنا .

13. Certainly Taj Mahal is beautiful.

١٣ . إن تاج محل جميل .

14. It pleases me to participate in this function.

١٤ . يسرنى أن اشترك فى هذه الحفلة .

15. As if the moon was a lamp in the desert.

١٥ . كأنَّ القمر مصباح فى الصحراء .

16. Would that, medicine is useful.

١٦ . ليت الدواء مفيد .

17. Perhaps the culprit is free.

١٧ . لعل المجرم طليق .

18. It pains me that the war is continuing.

١٨ . يولمنى أن الحرب مستمرة .

19. Certainly spring is not far off.

١٩ . إن الربيع غير بعيد .

20. The rain stopped but the flood is strong.

٢٠ . إمتنع المطر لكن الفيضان عظيم .

21. Perhaps the goal is near.

٢١ . لعل الهدف قريب .

22. None who consults in his affairs is repentant.

٢٢ . لا مستشير فى أموره نادما .

23. No jealous person is comfortable.

٢٣ . لا حاسد مستريحا .

24. The book is small but its utility is great.

٢٤ . الكتاب صغير لكن نفعه عظيم .

LESSON TWENTYTWO

THE NUMERALS, DAYS AND MONTHS

اسماء العدد والايام والشهور

CARDINALS

ten عَشَرَةُ	eleven أَحَدَ عَشَرَ	one واحِدُ
twenty عِشْرُون	twelve إِثنا عَشَرَ	two إِثنان
thirty ثَلاثُونَ	thirteen ثلاثة عَشَرَ	three ثَلاثَةُ
forty أَربَعُون	fourteen أربعة عشر	four أَربَعَةُ
fifty خَمْسُونَ	fifteen خمسة عشر	five خَمْسَةُ
sixty سِتُّونَ	sixteen ستة عشر	six سِتَّةُ
seventy سَبْعُونَ	seventeen سبعة عشر	seven سَبْعَةُ
eighty ثَمَانُونَ	eighteen ثمانية عشر	eight ثَمَانِيةُ
ninety تِسْعُونَ	nineteen تسعة عشر	nine تِسْعَةُ
hundred مائَةُ	twenty عِشرونَ	ten عَشَرَةُ

400 أَربَعُ مِئةٍ	300 ثَلاثُ مئةٍ	200 مائَتانِ
700 سَبْعُ مِئةٍ	600 سِتُّ مئةٍ	500 خَمْس مئةٍ
1000 أَلف	900 تِسْعُ مِئةٍ	800 ثَمائى مئةٍ

ORDINALS

	Feminine مؤنث	Masculine مذكر
first	الاولى	الاول
second	الثانية	الثانى
third	الثالثة	الثالث
fourth	الرابعة	الرابع
fifth	الخامسة	الخامس
sixth	السادسة	السادس
seventh	السابعة	السابع
eighth	الثامنة	الثامن
ninth	التاسعة	التاسع
tenth	العاشرة	العاشر

ربع   نصف   ثلث   خمس   سدس   واحد فى المائة   مائة فى المائة

$$\frac{1}{4} \qquad \frac{1}{2} \qquad \frac{1}{3} \qquad \frac{1}{5} \qquad \frac{1}{6} \qquad \%1 \qquad \%100$$

NOTE ON THE SYNTAX OF NUMERALS

1. (1 - 2) The numerals 1 and 2 agree in gender with the noun to which they refer. e.g. ولد واحد *one boy* بنت واحدة *one girl.*

2. (3 - 10) These numerals disagree in gender with the singular of the noun counted, and put that noun in the genitive plural.

e.g. ثلاثة أولاد *three boys*; ثلاث بنات *three girls.*

3. (11 - 12) Both parts of these numerals agree in gender with the noun. And the noun numbered is put in the accusative singular. e.g.

eleven women إحدى عشرة إمرأةٌ ; *eleven men* أحد عشر رجلاً

4. (13 - 19) These govern the noun in the accusative singular. The unit disagrees in gender with its noun and with the word for "ten". e.g.

thirteen women. ثلاث عشرة إمرأةٌ ; *thirteen men* ثلاثة عشر رجلا

أيام الأسبوع WEEK DAYS

Wednesday	٤ . يَومُ الأربعاء	Sunday	١ . يَومُ الاحد
Thursday	٥ . يَومُ الخميس	Monday	٢ . يَومُ الاثنين
Friday	٦ . يوم الجمعة	Tuesday	٣ . يَومُ الثلاثاء
Saturday	٧ . يوم السبت		

MONTHS OF THE HIJRI YEAR «العربية» الشهور الهجرية

٧ . رجب	١ . محرم
٨ . شعبان	٢ . صفر
٩ . رمضان	٣ . ربيع الاول
١٠ . شوال	٤ . ربيع الثانى
١١ . ذو القعدة	٥ . جمادى الاولى
١٢ . ذو الحجة	٦ . جمادى الثانية

MONTHS OF THE CHRISTIAN YEAR «الميلادية» الشهور

	Used in Syria	Used in Egypt
January	كانون الثانى	١ . يناير
February	شباط	٢ . فبراير
March	آذار	٣ . مارس

	Used in Syria		Used in Egypt
April	نيسان		٤ . أبريل
May	أيار		٥ . مايو
June	حزيران		٦ . يونيو
July	تموز		٧ . يوليو
August	آب		٨ . اغسطس
September	ايلول		٩ . سبتمبر
October	تشرين الاول		١٠ . اكتوبر
November	تشرين الثانى		١١ . نوفمبر
December	كانون الاول		١٢ . ديسمبر

الوقت TIME

five minutes past nine	التاسعة وخمس دَقائق	One o'clock	الساعة الواحدة
twenty minutes past eleven	الحادية عشرة وعشرون دَقائق	quarter past one	الواحدة والربع
half past seven	السابعة والنصف	half past one	الواحدة والنصف
quarter to nine	التاسعة إلا الربع	quarter to two	الثانية إلا الربع

TYPES OF NOUNS DERIVED FROM VERBS

تقسيم الاسم إلى مصدر، وجامد ومشتق

Nouns and its varieties have been dealt with in the earlier lessons of this book. The discussion in this lesson concerns nouns derived from the verbs, which come very near to what are known as Gerund and Participle in English.

Arab Grammarians have classified Nouns into three groups.

1. اسم المصدر "The Verbal Noun" which properly expresses the verbal idea in the form of a noun. It is the root (of a word) from which proceed the verb and its derivatives. The radical letters of verbs are adopted from it.

e.g.	صَوْتٌ	سَيْرٌ	اضْطِرابٌ	إمْتِنَاع	حِرْفَةٌ
	sound	walking	striking	forbidding	profession

	فَرَحُ	فَصَاحَةٌ	سُهُولَةٌ	مَرَضٌ	لَوْنٌ
	happiness	eloquence	easiness	malady	colour

	مَوقِع	مَوعِد	زِراعَة	فَتْحُ	قُعُود
	situation	engagement	agriculture	opening	sitting

2. الاسم الجامد It is a noun which is "stationary" or "incapable of growth". In other words it is a noun which is neither derived from any word nor any word is derived from it. e.g.

فرس	رجل	جعفر
horse	man	Jafar

3. الاسم المشتق It is a noun which is derived from a verbal root. The following are formed from the verb فتح to open

فاتح	مفتوح	مفتاح
opener	opened	key

There are six forms of nouns which are derived from the verbal root.

1. Active participle	إسم الفاعل
2. Passive participle	إسم المفعول
3. Adjectives which are assimilated to the Active participles	الصفة المشبهة باسم الفاعل
4. The noun of pre-eminence	إسم التفضيل
5. The Noun denoting instruments	إسم الآلة
6. The Noun of time or place	إسم الزمان والمكان

The nouns which the Arab Grammarians call اسم الفاعل *Active participle* and اسم المفعول *Passive participle*, are verbal adjectives, i.e. adjectives derived from verbs, and nearly correspond in meaning to what are known as participles in the English language. A nominal sentence which consists of a subject and a predicate generally has either of these as predicate.

1. THE ACTIVE PARTICIPLE اسم الفاعل

It denotes the person who does the act or is responsible for it. It is formed from the verb in the past tense, 3rd person, by adding Alif after the first radical and giving kasrah ِ to the second radical. There are some exceptions to this rule, e.g.

سَمِيع	كَرِيم	رَسُول	فاعِل	كاتِب	عالِم
hearer	*generous*	*messenger*	*doer*	*writer*	*knower*

2. THE PASSIVE PARTICIPLE اسم المفعول

It denotes the person or a thing towards which the action is extended. It is formed by prefixing م with Fathah َ to the verb in the past tense, 3rd person, and adding و after the second radical, e.g.

مَفعول	مَكْتوب	مَعْلوم	مَجهول
a thing done	*written*	*known*	*unknown*

3. ADJECTIVES WHICH ARE ASSIMILATED TO THE ACTIVE PARTICIPLE

الصفة المشبهة باسم الفاعل

This is formed from the intransitive verb. It expresses a quality inherent and permanent in a person or thing without any limitation. It is used with a view to convey a certain degree of intensity. In this respect it is slightly different from اسم الفاعل *the active participle.* e.g.

hard   صُلْبُ (صلب)   handsome   حَسَنُ (حَسُنَ)   red   أُحْمَر (حُمْر)

noble   شريف (شرف)   brave   شُجاعُ (شَجَعَ)   black   اسود (سود)

4. THE NOUN OF PRE-EMINENCE AND DEGREES OF COMPARISON

اسم التفضيل

This is used when it is intended to express that one person surpasses others in possessing a certain quality. The following sentences illustrate the degrees of comparison; in the last two sentences the superlative degree is used.

1. Knowledge is more useful than wealth.	١ . العلم أنفع من المال .
2. The elephant is bulkier than the camel.	٢ . الفيل أضخم من الجمل .
3. The aeroplane is faster than the train.	٣ . الطيارة أسرع من القطار .
4. The West is more advanced than the East.	٤ . الغرب أكثر تقدما من الشرق .
5. Zaid is most learned.	٥ . زيد علامة .
6. God is most merciful.	٦ . الله رحيم .

5. THE NOUN DENOTING THE INSTRUMENT OF THE ACT   اسم الآلة

A noun which denotes the instrument that one uses in performing the act (expressed by a verb) is called in Arabic, اسم الآلة. This is formed by prefixing with Kasrah ـِ, to the verb in the past tense, 3rd person. It has three different forms.

a stick	مِضْرَبٌ	a plough	مِزْرَعٌ	a needle	مِخْيَطٌ	١. مِفْعَلٌ ـ
a net	مِصْيَدَةٌ	a broom	مِكْنَسَةٌ	a fan	مِرْوَحَةٌ	٢. مِفْعَلَةٌ ـ
a lamp	مِصْباحٌ	a saw	مِنْشارٌ	a key	مِفْتاحٌ	٣. مِفْعالٌ ـ

6. NOUN OF PLACE OR TIME   اسم الظرف

A noun which indicates the time or place of occurrence of the act is called in Arabic اسم الظر ف. This is formed by prefixing م with Fathah ﹷ to the verb in the past tense, 3rd person, e.g.

مَسْجِد	مَغْرِب	مَشْرِق
where prayer is offered *(mosque)*	where the sun sets *(west)*	where the sun rises *(east)*

مَوْعِد	مَنْزِل	مَجْلِس
the time or place of promise/*engagement*	place of landing *(residence)*	place of gathering *(assembly)*

LESSON TWENTYFOUR

DERIVED FORMS OF THE VERB   الفعل المجرد والمزيد فيه

The great majority of the Arabic verbs are triliteral, i.e. they consist of three radical letters only. The quadriliteral verbs, which consist of four radical letters are less in number.

The triliteral verbs are of two kinds :

(1) Those which contain merely the three radical letters which are known as الثلاثى المجرد e.g. خرج *to go out.*

(2) Those which contain one, two or three additional letters, besides the three radical letters. These are known as الثلاثى المزيد فيه e.g.

أخـرج *to send out.* These in fact are "the derived forms of the trilite-ral verbs." They differ from the original, in meaning, to some extent. In the Arabic dictionaries, the triliteral verb as such finds the first place and the meanings of its derived forms follow one by one.

The derived forms of the triliteral verbs are twelve in number :

A. Forms increased by one letter :

١. افعل خَرَجَ ـ أَخْرَجَ	٢. فعّل ضَرَبَ ـ ضَرَّبَ
٣. فاعل قَتَلَ ـ قَاتَلَ	

B. Forms increased by two letters :

٤. تفعّل قَبِلَ ـ تَقَبَّلَ	٥. تفاعل قَتَلَ ـ تَقَاتَلَ
٦. افتعل جَنَبَ ـ إِجْتَنَبَ	٧. انفعل فطَرَ ـ إِنْفَطَرَ
٨. افعلّ حَمِرَ ـ إِحْمَرَّ	

C. Forms increased by three letters :

٩. افعالَّ دَهَمَ ـ إِدْهَامَّ	١٠. استفعل نَصَرَ ـ إِسْتَنْصَرَ
١١. افعوعل خَشَنَ ـ إِخْشَوْشَنَ	١٢. افعوّل جَلَذَ ـ إِجْلَوَّذَ

Details about each of the above forms of derived verbs :

I. أَفْعَلَ ـ This is formed by prefixing Hamza أ as a result of which the first radical loses its vowel. It implies causing an act.

to make one sit أَجْلَسَ   *to sit* جَلَسَ

* ١. أَجْلَسَ   ٢. يُجْلِسُ   ٣. أَجْلِسْ   ٤. لَاتُجْلِسْ   ٥. إِجْلَاسًا

٦. مُجْلِسٌ   ٧. مُجْلَسٌ

II. فَعَّلَ ـ The second form is formed by doubling the second radical. It implies that an act is done with intensity.

to teach عَلَّمَ   *to know* عَلِمَ

١. عَلَّمَ   ٢. يُعَلِّمُ   ٣. عَلِّمْ   ٤. لَاتُعَلِّمْ   ٥. تَعْلِيمًا   ٦. مُعَلِّمٌ

٧. مُعَلَّمٌ

III. فَاعَلَ ـ This is formed by the introduction of Alif after the first radical. This expresses the effort to perform the act upon the object.

to try to kill قَاتَلَ   *to kill* قَتَلَ

١. قَاتَلَ   ٢. يُقَاتِلُ   ٣. قَاتِلْ   ٤. لَاتُقَاتِلْ   ٥. مُقَاتَلَةً

٦. مُقَاتِلٌ   ٧. مُقَاتَلٌ

IV. تَفَعَّلَ ـ This is formed by prefixing ت and doubling the 2nd radical. This adds reflexive force to the original verb.

to be broken to pieces تكَسَّر   *to break* كَسَر

١. تَكَسَّرَ   ٢. يَتَكَسَّرُ   ٣. تَكَسَّرْ   ٤. لَاتَتَكَسَّرْ   ٥. تَكَسُّرًا

٦. مُتَكَسِّر   ٧. مُتَكَسَّر

---

*Under each form of the derived verbs, the following are shown : (1) Past tense (2) Imperfect (3) Imperative (4) Negative command (5) Verbal noun : gerund (6) Active participle noun (7) Passive participle noun.

V. تفاعل - This is formed by prefixing ت and by adding "Alif" before the second radical. The idea of reflexive action is conveyed by this form.

to fight one another تقاتل   *to kill* قتل

١. تَقَاتَلَ ٢. يَتَقَاتَلُ ٣. تَقَاتَلْ ٤. لاتَقَاتَلْ ٥. تَقَاتُلاً

٦. مُتَقَاتِلٌ ٧. مُتَقَاتَلٌ

VI. افتعل - This is formed by prefixing إ "Hamzat al wasal" and adding ت after the first radical which loses its vowel thereby.

to avoid إجْتَنَبَ   *to set apart* جنب

١. إجْتَنَبَ ٢. يَجْتَنِبُ ٣. إجْتَنِبْ ٤. لاتَجْتَنِبْ ٥. إجْتِنَاباً

٦. مُجْتَنِبٌ ٧. مُجْتَنَبٌ

VII. انفعل - This is formed by prefixing إ and ن. It has a reflexive signification. It is generally used as a passive.

to be split إنفطر   *to create* فطر

١. إنْفَطَرَ ٢. يَنْفَطِرُ ٣. إنْفَطِرْ ٤. لاتَنْفَطِرْ ٥. إنْفِطَاراً

٦. مُنْفَطِرُ

VIII. افعلَّ - This is formed by prefixing إ "Hamzat al wasal" and doubling the third radical. It is used to express colours and defects.

to become red إحمرَّ   *to make red* حمر

١. إحْمَرَّ ٢. يَحْمَرُّ ٣. إحْمَرِرْ ٤. لاتَحْمَرِرْ ٥. إحْمِراراً

٦. مُحْمَرٌّ

IX. افعالَّ - This is formed by prefixing "Hamzah" إ and adding 'Alif' after the second radical and doubling the third. This too is used to express colours.

to be black إِدْهامَّ   *to blacken* دهم

١ . إِدْهامَّ ٢ . يَدْهامُّ ٣ . إِدْهامِمْ ٤ . لاتَدْهامِمْ ٥ . إِدْهِيْمَاما
٦ . مُدْهامٌّ

X. اِسْتَفْعَل ـ This is formed by prefixing إ س ت This too has a reflexive signification and is used when an object is sought.

to call for help إِسْتَنْصَرَ   *to help* نصر

١ . إِسْتَنْصَرَ ٢ . يَسْتَنْصِرُ ٣ . إِسْتَنْصِرْ ٤ . لاتَسْتَنْصِرْ ٥ . إِسْتِنْصاراً
٦ . مُسْتَنْصِرٌ ٧ . مُسْتَنْصَرُ

Forms No. XI and XII are used only occasionally.

THE QUADRILITERAL VERBS

The verbs which contain four radical letters are called رباعى. These are of two kinds :

I. Those which consists of merely four radicals and are known as

المجرد الرباعى .

II. Those which consist of one or two letters besides the four radicals.

Examples of the first category :

دَحْرَجَ   وَسْوَسَ   زَلْزَلَ   جَمْهَرَ   هَرْوَلَ
to roll   *to whisper*   *to shake*   *to collect*   *to rush*

١ . دَحْرَجَ ٢ . يُدَحْرِجُ ٣ . دَحْرِجْ ٤ . لاتُدَحْرِجْ ٥ . دَحْرَجَةً
٦ . مُدَحْرِجُ ٧ . مُدَحْرَجُ

The derived forms of the quadriliteral verbs are :

١ . تَفَعْلَلَ (تَدَحْرَجَ) ٢ . افْعَنْلَلَ (إحْرَنْجَمَ) ٣ . افْعَلَلَّ (إقْشَعَرَّ)

LESSON TWENTYFIVE

THE PARTICLES - A SUMMARY الحروف

There are four kinds of particles حروف : (1) Prepositions, (2) Adverbs, (3) Conjunctions and (4) Interjections as they are understood in English.

CONJUNCTIONS حروف العطف

The conjunctions are either (a) Separable or (b) Inseparable.

(a) The examples of separable conjunctions are لكِنْ *but,* ثُمَّ *then, thereupon.*

(b) ف and و *and* are very widely used as conjunction. They do not stand alone but are prefixed to Nouns, Pronouns, Particles and Verbs as well.

INTERJECTIONS حروف النداء

The particles which are widely used as Interjections are يا and يٰاأَيُّها meaning "Oh" e.g. ياولد *Oh boy,* ياأَيُّها المؤمنون *Oh the faithful!*

VOCABULARY OF PARTICLES

Prepositions and words which are used as such:

to	لِ	within	داخل	to : until	إلى
at, with	لَدَى	without	دُونَ	in front, before	أمام
from	مِنْ	on, above	عَلَى	with, by	بِ
without	مِنْ غَيْرِ	of, from, about	عَنْ	after	بَعْدَ
since	مَنْذُ	with	عِنْدَ	between, among	بَيْنَ
with	مَعَ	instead of	عِوَض	by (in swearing)	تَ
by (in swearing)	وَ	except	غير	under	تَحْتَ
behind	وَراءُ	in	فى	next, near	جَنْب
middle	وَسَطُ	above	فَوْق	until, even to	حَتَّى

| besides | سِوَى | before (time) | قَبْل | round, around | حَوْل |
| after, behind | خَلْف | opposite | قُدَّام | outside | خارِج |

ADVERBS

(a) The adverbs which are used as interrogatives are mentioned in lesson No. 13.

(b) *Adverbs of Place :*

here	هاهُنا	here	هُنا	outside	بَرَّا
on top	فَوْق	there	هُناك	inside	جَوَّا
down, below	تَحْت	there	هُنالِكَ	wherever	أيْنَما

(c) *Adverbs of time :*

now	الآن	early	بُكْرَة	today	اليَوم
at any time	قَطّ	late	مُتَأَخِّرا	yesterday	البارِحَة
immediately	مُباشَرَة	ever, never	أبَداً	day before yesterday	أوّل البارِحة
directly					
to-morrow	غَداً	always	دائِما	yesterday	أمس
afterwards	بَعْدُ	immediately	حالاً	earlier	سابِقاً

(d) *Adverbs of Quality :*

| without | بِدُون | little | شُوَيَّة | very, much | كثير |
| enough | كِفَاية | little | قَليل | much, most | جِدّاً |

(e) *Adverbs of Affirmation and Negation :*

| together with | مَعاً | thus, so | كَذا | yes | نَعْم |
| nearly | تَقْريباً | together with | جَميعاً | thus, so | هكذا |

LESSON TWENTYSIX

THE VERBS OF PRAISE AND BLAME   افعال المدح والذم

THE FORMS EXPRESSIVE OF SURPRISE AND WONDER   افعال التعجب

The verbs of praise and blame are نِعْمَ *to be good* and بِئس *to be bad.* نِعم is used to express a high degree of appreciation. بِئسَ is used to express blame, e.g.

1. An excellent friend is the book	١ . نعم صديقاً الكتاب
2. He who relies on other than himself is blame worthy.	٢ . بِئسَ رجلا مَن يعتمد على سواه

Besides نعم and بئس the expression used for praise is حَبَّذا and the word used for blame is ساء

THE FORMS EXPRESSIVE OF SURPRISE OR WONDER   افعال التعجب

In order to express surprise or wonder, two expressions are used in Arabic, which are called : افعال التعجب *The verbs of Surprise or Wonder.*These are (1) ما التعجبية "the Mä that expresses surprise" ; (2) the use of the Imperative tense, singular, masculine followed by the preposition. بِ Examples of these two forms are given below.

The first is on the pattern	ما أُفعلَهُ .
The second is on the pattern	أُفعِل بِهِ .
1. How pleasant the spring season is!	١ . ما أُحسنَ فصل الربيع .
2. How great is India's industrial progress!	٢ . أُعِظمْ بِتقدم صناعة الهند .

الكتب اصدقاؤنا   سهير قلماوى

١. التفكير ميزة الانسان والكتب أداة التفكير

إن ما يُمَيِّزُ الانسان من الحيوان هو التفكير ـ وإن بعض الحيوان لَيُفكِّر بدرجة من الدرجات ولكن تفكير الانسان أرقى ـ وهو يصعد فى سلم الرقى بقفرات تعلو و تعلو أبدا ـ وسبيل هذا الصعود هو أن يَبْنى الخلف على آثار السلف مما لا يمكن ان يتم فى عالم الحيوان وإنما يتم فى عالم الانسان ليس غير

ولا يمكن لهذا البناء أن يتم إلا بواسطة الكتب فالكتب هى التى يمكن لها أن تدلنا على الدرج الذى ارتقى إليه الاقدمون لنرقى نحن فى ما بعد ـ إنها هى التى تُوفِّر علينا الجهد فى أن نبدأ من جديد فى كل ميدان من ميادين العلم أو المعرفة .

٢. رسالة الكتب

إن رسالة الكتب ترمى إلى أهداف ثلاثة : أماالهدف الاول فهو أن تُعلِّمنا ما لا نعلم والهدف الثانى أن توحى إلينا بما نحتاج إليه فى الحياة، وأما الأخير فهو أن تَسمو بمشاعرنا ومداركنا إلى ما يجب أن نسمو إليه من رفعة وطهر .

إن الكتب تعلمنا الحرفة التى نريد أن نحترفها مثلا وتعلمنا ماذا يمكن أن نفيد من تجارب غيرنا فى هذه الحرفة بالذات، وماذا يمكن أن ننتفع به من تجارب من سَبقونا، وكيف يمكن أن نبعث الحياة فى ما نعلم بحيث يحيا من جديد وننفع به أنفسنا و من حولنا.

حتى قرأة شعر من المتشائمين من الشعراء تفيد لانها ترينا أن الحياة التى نحياها إذا ما قسناها بحياتهم، أفضل منها و أليق بأن تبعث النشاط والأمل ـ أما شعر المتفائلين فهو بدوره ينعشنا ويجعل نور الحياة يَتَوهَّج فى أعيننا و ينتشر ضياؤه.

لولا الكتب لمرت بنا مناظر القرى رَتيبَة [المتصبة بالثياب وعدم التحرك أو التغير] فارغة، بائسة يائسة لا توحى بشئ ـ إنها مجرد ألوان وخطوط وظلال تتلاقى وتفترق ولا تترك فى الخيال إلا ما يتركه المنظر العابر، يراه الطفل من خلف زُجاج نافذة القطار وهو يعبُر به الريف الخالد من مكان إلى مكان.

فائدة القراءة

القراءة مُتْعَةً [لذة وإفادة] عظيمة بسعر رخيص وهى فى الوقت نفسه لتفيد الانسان بزمان أو   مكان فهو يستطيع أن يقرأ وَقْتما يريد، وأينما يحلو له ـ ولقد كان السَّماع فى قديم الزمان يقوم مقام القراءة، وكانت أخبار أبطال القدماء ومغامراتهم تُقصُّ على الناس شفاها. فالالياذة [ملحمة : أى قصة شعرية يونانية] والف ليلة وليلة [مجموعة قصص تصور الحياة فى البلاد الشرقية] وسيرة عنترة [قصة شعبية تدور حوادثها حول حياة الشاعر الفارس الجاهلى عنترة، ويتخللها كثير من الاشعار] كلها قصص تاريخى أو خيالى، كانت تُنشَد للجمهور على آلة موسيقية ليسمع ويطرب لما يسمع ـ ولكن العصر الحديث يقدم لنا هذا القصص و الخيال الشعرى كله بين دَفَّتى كتاب [الدفة : الجنب من كل شئ أو صفحة] والكتاب الحديث منشد عصرى يحدثك أويغنيك بالطريقة التى تُلائم عصرك، ولكنه دائما ابدا، رغم الصمت فى حروف الطبع، يُحادثك من خلال ما تقرأ، فَيُسَلِّى وحدتك ويمتعك ويعلمك ويلَذُّ لك،

و من بين دَفَّتى الكتاب تَتَعَرَّف إلى أبطال أقرب إلى القلب من أبطال الحياة : إنهم أكمل و أكثر إنسانية و أقرب إلى النفس ـ لذالك تستطيع أن تكون بينك وبينهم صداقات لا يمكن أن يتاح لك تكوينها مع أبطال الحياة ـ إنهم أقرب وأيسر منالا ، بل هم طوع إشارتك ، تتقدم إليهم إذا شئت ، ويُحَدِّثُك عنهم أقرب الناس إليهم ، أو هم أنفسهم ، فاذا أنت تعرف عنهم مالا يمكن أن تعرفه عن بطل الحياة ـ

إن الكتب لينة طَيِّعة ، حلوة الطبع رقيقة المعشر ، فخذ منها ما تأخذ ودَع منها ما تدَع ، ولا تُرغِم نفسك بأى حال. من الاحوال على قراءة ما لا تحب ـ خذ الكتاب فى انشراح وبسطة أسارير [وبسط الأسارير ، مع انفراجها دلالة على السرور و الانشراح] واعلم دأما أنك تستطيع أن تتركه متى شئت ، و أن تُغَيِّره إلى ما تُحب .

أُحمـد أمـين   طريق النجاح

قوة الارادة : الوراثة والبيئة لهما أثر كبير فى تحديد حياة الإنسان و توجيهها،
ولكنّ إرادة الانسان، و عزمه القوىّ قادران على التغلب على عقبات [الطرق
الصعبة] الوراثه والبيئة، وكل إنسان يستطيع خلق حياته بأسمة أو شقية متى
ظفر بالطموح، والارادة الغالبة، والتفكير الصحيح ـ

طريق النجاح : وعلى الانسان ألا ييأس ـ وليتسع أمله، ويتوقع الخير،
فبذلك يستطيع أن ينمّى معارفه وخبراته، ويصل إلى ما يرجو، و لا يتعلَّل
[أبدى الحجة و تمسك بها] بأنه ليس نابغة، أو الظروف لا تسمح له بالنجاح،
فالحياة ليست وقفا على النابغين وحدهم.

ومن الناس ـ مَن يعتقد أن فريقا من الناس قد مُنحوا القدرة على التفوق
والاتيان بالعجائب من غير مشقة، و هذه أفكار تُبعدُ عن النّجاح المنشود، فكل
مَن سار فى طريق العمل بدأ حياته حِذرا ـ ومن كان ذا قدرة على العمل نجح،
وكلما سار خطوة فى طريقة تابع سيره من غير خوف أو ملل أو تشكُّك أو
تعجُّل، حتى يصل إلى غايته.

الامل : وخير وسيلة للنجاح أن يكون للانسان أمل يطمح إليه، فيودُ أن
يكون عالما أو صانعا أو فنانا عظيما، فمن رضى بالقليل لم يصل إلى شيئ، و من
رسم لنفسه غرضا يسعى إليه، واجتهد فى بلوغه، نجح فى حياته ـ

عوامل الاخفاق : ومن أكبر أسباب الفشل فى الحياة : خلق الأعذار والأوهام
وسوءُ الظن، وتخذيل النفس، [التخذيل : الحمل على الفشل] واالشك فى

العاقبة والخوف من الفشل ـ ذلك كله يحجب عن العين نور النجاح ـ

النجاح المنشود : ويجب ألا يكون جمع المال وحده هو ما يَنشُده الشباب الطموح، وأن يجعل السعى إليه طريق الاحتيال واستغلال الآخرين، والنجاح المؤسس على ذلك نجاح رخيص ـ

إنما النجاح المنشود : أن يجمع الانسان مع نجاحه فى العمل نبل الخلق، والصدق، والامانة والعطف والتسامح وبِرَّ الضعفاء [أحسن معاملته فى حب] وذوى الحاجة. فالناس قد خلقوا لتبادل المنافع والخير لا ليستغلهم القادرون.

ومن الخطأ أن يقوَّمَ نجاح الشخص بما حصل عليه من مال فخير المجتمع فى شاب أقام مَثَلَه الاعلى على الأخلاق يسير عليها، وليس فى آخر لعل غايته فى الحياة المال وتخطِّى رقاب الناس فليس غاية الانسان فى حياته أن يجمع المال ليأكل ويشرب ما لذَّ من الطعام والشراب بل غايته : أن يستمتع بحب الخير ويدرك جمال الدنيا وجمال العقل والقول، ويشعر بسموّ أحاسيسه ـ

وليس الغاية من ذلك تثبيط همم الشباب عن الرغبة فى النجاح المادى بل يجب محاربة الزهد والركون فى الحياة [ركن الشيئى : مال إليه] إلى الكسل والخمول والحظ والمصادفة، ويجب أن يقترن النجاح المادى بالعمل لصالح المجتمع ورفعته وبالخلق القويم.

الثقة بالنفس : ومن أهم عوامل النجاح الثقة بالنفس والايمان بانها قادرة على الكفاح والنجاح، ومن الخطأ أن يحتقر الانسان نفسه ويحسب أنه غير قادر على شيئ ويبتعد عن الطموح ولْيعلم أن الناس يحتقرون من احتقر نفسه ويدوسون من استذل ـ

ومن الخطأ أن يخلِطَ الانسان بين الثقة بالنفس واحترامها وبين الكِبر

والغرور، فالثقة بالنفس الاعتقاد بقدرتها على تحمل الأعباء والكبر والغرور أن يعطى الانسان نفسه أكثر مما تستحق ويطالب بالجزاء من غير عمل، وخداع الناس بالمظاهر الكاذبة.

الابتسام والتفاؤل : وعلى الانسان أن يحيا متفائلا لينشط عقله وتتبدد متاعبه [تزول متاعبه] فالمتفائلون خير الناس صحة، وأقدرهم على الجِدّ فى العمل وأقربهم إلى النجاح وأكثرهم إفادة من الحياة.

عوامل النجاح : إن طريق النجاح : أن يتّسع أفق الانسان ويحدّد مَثَله الاعلى ويثق بنفسه، ويبتعد عن الكبرياء والغرور ويبتسم للحياة. من سار فى حياته فى هذا السبيل كان خيرا لأمته ولنفسه وكان ناجحا فى حياته ولو لم يكسب مالا كثيرا.

الحرية غذاء الشباب   ميخائيل نعيمة

ليس الشباب فى حاجة إلى مَن يوجِّهه ـ فالقوى الهائلة التى يذخر بها كيانه هى الكفيلة بِتَوجيهِه فى السبيل المعدِّ له ـ وإنما حاجة الشباب إلى مَن يحميه من مُوَجهيه الذين يحاولون أن يَكمُّوا فاه ، ويُكبلوا يَديه ورجليه ويَسكبوا الماء البارد على الحماسة الملتهبة فى صدره ، ويزرَعوا الذعر والخُنوع فى فكره وقلبه ـ أولئك الذين يعيشون فى قلق دائم من ثورة الشباب على مارثً من التقاليد ، وما بلى من الاساليب ـ ولذلك لاينفكون يقيمون السدود والحواجز فى وَجه تفتُّح الشباب وانطلاقِه ـ وهم إذ يفعلون ذلك لا يدركون إلى أى حد يسيئون إلى أنفسِهم وإلى الشباب .

٢ ـ الشباب ربيع : فمثلَما لاخير فى أرض ربيعها خريف أو شتاء كذلك لاخير فى أمة شبابها كهولة أو شيخوخة وإنه لمن الاثم الذى لايغتفر أن نمسك على الشباب حرية الافصاح عما فى نفسه من قوى تتحفز للوثوب ، فنجعله يَدُبُّ (يمشى على اليدين والرجلين) حيث يستطيع أن يطير ، ونجعله يتردد حيث يطلب الانطلاق .

فالشباب ربيعُنا ، ومن حقِّنا أن ننعم به متفجرا من أعماقنا ، كما ننعم بالربيع متفجرا من أحشاء الارض فلا يُحوّل ورده قُطرُبا (نبات شائك) وياسمينه عوسجا وبلابله غربانا ، ونسوره بُوما ـ وذلك ما نفعَله عندما نَحرِمُ الشباب حُرِّية التعبير عن نفسه إن بالقول أو بالفعل ـ ثم نحضُره فى قوالب صُلبة قاسية لاتلبثُ أن تضيق به فتتشقق وتتطايرَ شظايا تدميه و تُدمينا على السواء ، وقد تُهلكه وتهلكنا ـ

٣ ـ والشباب ثروة : إن ثروة الشباب هى فى صفاء بَصَره وبَصيرته ، وفى

مضاء عزيمته، وفى ثورته على الركود والجمود ـ وهذه الصفات هى التى تُميز الشباب من غير الشباب، والتى لولاها لما جرى مَركب فى بحر، ولا اشتَعَلتْ نار فى دار، ولا خاطت إبرة ثوبا، ولا شُيّد حجر فوق حجر، ولا كانَ لنا أى علم أو فنّ أو نظام، ولا أى شىءٍ من الاشياء التى بها نعيش ومنها تألفت مدنياتنا الغابرة وتتألف الحاضرة، وستتألف التى بعدها ـ

شبابنا هو الثروة التى أين منها ذهَبُنا الاسود (البترول) والأصفر وكل ما تنتجه أرضنا من ثمار وحبوب؟ هذه للنفاد والبَوار، وتلك للبقاء والازدهار ـ وحرى بنا أن نستثمر هذه الثروة إلى أقصى حد، ونوليها من عنايتنا أضعاف ما نوليه الدوالى فى كرومنا، والسنابل فى حقولنا ولا نقضى عليها بما نفرضه على الشباب من قيود، بل نطلق له حريةَ القول وحرية العمل إذا نحن شئنا أن ننعمَ بمواهبه وبركاته، وأن نتفادى غضباته وثوراته ـ

٤ ـ الحرية غذاؤه ـ ولا يقولن قائل إن تلك الحرية قد تؤدى بنا إلى الفوضى ـ فالفوضى هى مانحن فيه ـ ولن يخرجنا منها إلى الشباب المجدّد والمتجدّد ـ ويقينى أن ما فى دم شبابنا من حرارة، وما فى عقله من اتزان، وما فى قلبه من إيمان بالعدل والنظام والاخاء والحرية، لكفيل بان يقطع بنا شوطا بعيدا نحو عالم ألطَفَ جوا وأفسح أفقا، وأعذب صوتا من عالم نعيش فيه الآن ـ فليس كالشباب خزانة نأتمنها على آمالنا ـ وليس كالشباب مجدّاد لشباب الحياة ـ وليس كالحرية غذاء للشباب وحافزا له على الابداع والسير بالقافلة إلى الواحات المطمئنة والمراعى الخصبة.

الدكتور أحمـد زكى   حيوانات أنَّسناها

١ ـ فى الزمن المقديم : لقد جاء على الدنيا زمان لم يكن فيه بها حيوان أنيس ـ
ولكنَّ هذا زمان قديم جدّاً ـ إن الناس تعلموا أن يُؤنِسوا الحيوانات فى هذا
الماضى البعيد، فى تلك الايام التى لم يكن فيها سلاح إلا ما يصنعونه من
الحجر، ولم تكن لهم كتابة إلا مَا يرسمونه من صور ـ

٢ ـ تأنيس الكلب : والكلب أول حيوان أنَّسه الانسان ـ وفى الزمن نفسه تقريبا
أنَّسَ الانسان البقرة والخنزير ـ والناس احتاجوا إلى الكلب أولا ليكون لهم
صاحبا ـ ولكنهم وجدوا أنه يستطيع أن ينفَعَهم وأن يحميهُم ـ إن الكلب ينبح عند
اقتراب عدوٍ فينبِّه أصحابه ـ

و بعد ذلك وجد الناس للكلاب منافع أخرى ـ أنَّسَ الناس حيوانات ، فوجدوا أن
الكلاب تستطيع أن تمنع هذه الحيوانات من الهرب ـ كذلك وجدوا ان الكلاب
تساعد فى صيد الحيوانات على البرِّ وفى صيد السمك فى الماء ووجدوا أنها
تستطيع جرَّ الاثقال ـ

٣ ـ انواع من الكلاب مختلفة : والكلاب التى أنَّسها الناس أولا كانت تشبه
الذئاب شبها كبيراً ـ ومن هذه الكلاب الأُولى جاءت بالولادة أنواع مختلفة من
الكلاب ، بعضها كبيرٌ ، وبعضها صغير كاللُّعب ، وبعضها له شَعر طويل ، وبعضها
له شعر قصير ، وبعضها يُعين الناس فى شيئ وبعضها يعين فى شيئ غيره ـ
والكلبة تلد فى العادة عددا من الجراء ، يختلف بين ستة جِراء وإثنى عشر
جَروا ـ وهى تطعمها من لبنها ـ

٤ ـ بين الابقار والكلاب : والابقار تختلف عن الكلاب اختلافا كبيرا ـ فالكلاب تأكل اللحمَ، والابقار تأكل النباتات ـ والابقار لها طريقة غربية فى أكل طعامها، وهو من نبات ـ فهى تأكله اولا أكلا سريعاً، فلا تمضغه، فينزل فى جوفها خشنا ـ ثم بعد ذلك، بعد أن يُطرّى فى جوفها، ترجعُ به إلى فمها، وعندئذ تمضغه. وعندئذ نقول إنها تجترُّ ـ

والكلاب لها أسنان تنفع فى تمزيق اللحم ـ والابقار لها أسنان تنفع فى قَضم النبات، وفى مَضغِه بعد ذلك ـ والكلاب لها مخالب، والابقار لها حوافر، وهى لها حافران فى القدم الواحدة ـ

والبقرة تلدُ فى العادة عجلا واحدا فى المرة الواحدة، وأحيانا تلد عجلين تَوأمَينِ؛ والعجل لايولد عاجزا كعجز الجرو، فهو لاتمرّ على ولادته أيام قليلة حتى يكون يجرى. وهو كالجرو، يعيش على اللبن يرضعه من أمه.

٥ ـ الشياه والمعيز : والشاة الاولى التى أنَّسناها لم يكن لها صوف كثيف ناعم كالذى لها الآن ـ وإنما كان لها شعر خشن غليظ ـ إن شِياهَنا اليوم لها صوف كثيف ناعم، نحن نجُزُّه ونصنع منه اقمشةٍ ـ نعمل منها ملابسنا الصوفية ـ وغير الصوف نأخذ من الشياه لحومها لنأكلها.

والمعيز والشياه أولاد أعمام ـ والشياه خوافة، ولا تخاف المعيزُ ـ ويطلق الناس عددا قليلا من المعيز التى لاتخاف مع الشياه لتحميَها من الحيوانات المتوحشة، ولتحفظ بها فلا تهرب والمعيز تحسِنُ تسلُّق الجبال، لهذا كثيرا ما تجدُ عند سكان الجبال قطعانا منها ـ

٦ ـ القطط : والقطط تشبه الكلاب أكثر مما تشبه حيوانا آخر من حيواناتنا المستأنسة وهى من آكلات اللحوم وهى تصحبنا فى المنازل فتُحسنُ صحبتنا، ونحن نُدللها، وهى تُعيننا بصيد الفئران والجرذان.

زِرياب المغنى   عبد الحميد العبادى

١ ـ شاعر، ولكنه إلى الشعر أميل :

كان أبو الحسن على بن نافع مولى للخليفة المهدى العباسى [عبدا من عبيده]ـ ولسواد لونه وحلاوة شمائله [حلاوة الطباع والخصال] لقّبوه بـ «زرياب» تشبيها له بطائر أسود غرد يُعرف عندهم بهذا الاسم ـ وقد تكاملت لزرياب كل أسباب النبوغ والتفوق موهوبها ومكسوبها فكان شديد الذكاء، لطيف الحسّ، شاعرا فصيح الشعر ـ غير أنه كان إلى الغناء أميَل وبه أشغَف ـ وقد درسه فى كتب الاقدمين من حكماء اليونان، وعلى أستاذه اسحق الموصلى زعيم المغنين فى ذلك الوقت ـ ولشدة إفتتان زرياب بالموسيقى كان تفكيره فيها لا يكاد ينقطع ـ حتى أنه كان يُلْهَمُ اللحن وهو نائم، فيهب من نومه مسرعا، ويدوّن ما وقع له، ثم يعود إلى مضجعه عَجِلا ومن ثَمّ [وهكذا] قيل إنه كان يأخذ ألحانه عن الجن .

٢ ـ هجرته إلى المغرب : ويذكرون أن السبب فى هجرة زرياب من المشرق إلى المغرب أنه غنى يوماً فى حضرة هارون الرشيد فاعجب الخليفةُ بفنه وظرفه ـ وطلب إلى إسحق الموصلىّ ان يُعنى به ـ ولكن إسحق لم يلبث أن تحركت فى صدره عوامل الغَيرة والحسد والحقد على تلميذه، فخلا به وخيّره بين الموت والحياة، بين أن يقيم ببغداد فيعرّض حياته للهلاك و بين أن يذهب فى أرض الله العريضة فينجوَ بحياته ـ ووعد إذا هو اختار ثانى الأمرين أن يعينه على الرحيل بما شاء من المال، وغير المال ـ فاختار زرياب الرحيل عن المشرق بأسره، ووفى له إسحق بما وعده به من المعونة ـ

٣ ـ احتفال عبد الرحمن لمقدمه : خرج زرياب مُيَمِّما وجهه شطر المغرب الاقصى [موجها وجهها نحو المغرب] ـ وهنا كتب إلى الحكم بن هشام، أمير الأندلس المعروف بحبه للموسيقى يستأذنه فى دخول الاندلس والصيرورة إليه [الذهاب إليه]، فأذن له الأمير فى كل ذلك من فوره ـ وعبر زرياب البحر إلى الأندلس ـ وبينما هو يتأهَّبُ للرحيل إلى قرطبة إذ سمع بوفاة الحكم، فهَمَّ أن يعود أدراجه إلى المشرق لو لا أن كتب إليه الأمير الجديد، عبد الرحمن الأوسط، يستقدُمه (يطلب إليه أن يأتى) ويعده أن يعطيه كل ما تصبو إليه نفسه من مال وجاه ـ فقدم عليه زرياب ـ ويروون أن عبد الرحمن احتفل لمقدمه أعظم إحتفال إذ خرج بنفسه من قرطبة لتلقّيه ـ وما هو إلا ان سمع غناءه وحديثه حتى شغف به، فغمره بفضله وإنعامه، وأجرى عليه من الرواتب والأرزاق الشئ الكثير وقدَّمه على سائر المغنين وبلغ من شدة شغفه به أن جعل فى قصره بابا خاصا يستدعيه منه كلما أحب سماع غناءه وحديثه العذب الطريف ـ

٤ ـ وفاء زرياب : وقد قابل زرياب النعمة بمثلها، وجزى المعروف بالمعروف ـ ولكنه قصد إلى ذلك من طريق غير مباشر، قصد إليه من طريق النصح والاخلاص للاندلس التى أصبحت له وطنا، وأهل الاندلس الذين أصبحوا أهلاً له، ومعشرا ـ فعكف على رفع مستوى الموسيقى الاندلسية، وعلى النهوض بالمجتمع الاندلسى حتى يدانى (يقارب) المجتمع الشرقى ببغداد ـ وقد وُفِّق فى ما قصد إليه كل التوفيق.

الإنسانية العامة   مصطفى لطفى المنفلوطى

١ . «ليس لصاحب وطن من الأوطان أو صاحب دين من الأديان أن يقول لغيره ممن يَسكُنُ وطنا غير وطنه، أو يدينُ بدينٍ غير دينه : أنا غيرُك، فيجب أن أكون عدوَّك ؛ لأن الإنسانية وحدة لا تكثر فيها ولا غَيرِيَّة ، ولأن هذه الفروق التى توجد بين الناس فى ارائهم ومذاهبهم، ومواطن إقامتهم وألوان أجسادهم وأطوالهم وأعراضهم ـ إنما هى اعتبارات ومصطلحات أو مصادفات واتفاقات، تعرضُ لجوهر الانسانية بعد تكوينه واستمام خلقه، وتتوارد عليه توارد الأعراض على الأجسام

٢ . وإذا جاز لكل إقليم أن يتنكر لغيره من الأقاليم جاز لكل بلد أن يتنكر لغيره من البلاد، بل جاز لكل بيت أن ينظر تلك النظرة الشزراء الى البيت الذى يجاوره، بل جاز للأب أن يقول لولده، وللولد أن يقول لأبيه : إليك عنّى لاتمد عينيك إلى شيٍ مما فى يدى، ولا تطمع على نفسى بشيٍ مما اختصتها به، لأنى غيرُك فيجب أن أكون عدوكَ المحارب لك، وهناك تنحلُّ كل عُقدةٍ، وتنفصم كل عُروة، ويحمل كل إنسان لأخيه بين اضلاعه من لواعج البُغض والمَقت ما يرنق عيشه، ويطيل سهده، ويقلق مضجعه، ويحبب إليه صورة الموت، ويبغض إليه وجه الحياة . وهنالك يُصبح الانسان أشبه بشيٍ بذلك الإنسان الأول فى وحشته وانفراده، يقلِّب وجهه فى آفاق السماء، وينبش بيديه طبقات الأرض، فلايجد فى الوحشة مؤنسا، ولا على الهموم معينا.

٣ . الجامعة الإنسانية أقرب الجامعات الى قلب الإنسان، وأعلقها بفؤاده، وألصقها بنفسه، لأنه يبكى لمصاب من لايعرف، وان كان ذلك المصاب تاريخا من التواريخ أو أسطورة من الأساطير، لأنه لايرى غريقايتخبط فى الماء أو حريقا يتلظى فى النار حتى تحدثه نفسه بالمخاطرة فى سبيله فيقف وقفة

الحزين المتلهف إن كان ضعيفا، ويندفع اندفاع الشجاع المستقتل ان كان قويا، ويسمع وهو بالشرق حديث النكبات بالغرب فيخفق قلبه، وتطير نفسه، لأنه يعلم أن أولئك المنكوبين إخوانه فى الإنسانية وإن لم يكن بينه وبينهم صلة فى أمر سواها، ولو لا أن ستارا من الجهل والعصبية يسبله كل يوم غلاة الوطنية والدين أو تجارهما على قلوب الضعفاء السذج لما عاش منكوب فى هذه الحياة بلا راحم، ولا ضعيف بلا معين.

٤. لابأس بالفكرة الوطنية، ولا بأس بالحمية الدينية، ولا بأس بالعصبية لهما، والذود عنهما، ولكن يجب أن يكون ذلك فى سبيل الإنسانية، وتحت ظلالها، أى أن تكون دوائر الجامعات كلها داخلة فى دائرة الإنسانية العامة، غير خارجة عنها.

والوطنية لاتزال عملا من الأعمال الشريفة المقدمة حتى تخرج عن حدود الإنسانية، فإذا هى خيالات باطلة، وأوهام كاذبة. والدين لازال غريزة من غرائز الخير المؤثرة فى صلاح النفوس وهداها، حتى يتجرد على الإنسانية وينابذها فإذا هو شعبة من شعب الجنون.

٥. فإن كان لابد للإنسان من أن يحاربَ أخاه أو يقاتلَه فليُحاربه مُدافعاً لا مهاجماً، وليقاتله مؤدِّبا لا منتقماً، وليكنْ موقفه أمامه فى جميع ذلك موقفَ العادل المنصفِ، والشقيق الرحيم، فيدفنه قتيلا، ويعالجه جريحاً، ويكرِمَه أسيراً، ويَخلُفه على أهله وولَدِه بأفضلِ ما يخلف الرجلُ الكريمُ أخاه الشقيق على ولَده من بعدِه، وليكنْ شأنه معه شأنَ تلك الفئة المتحاربة التى وصفها الشاعرُ بقوله:

إذا احترَبَتْ يوماً ففاضَتْ دِماؤُهَا   تَذَكَّرت القُربَى فَفاضَتْ دُموعُها

نــور الأنـدلس   أمين الريحانى

من حسنات الحياة زيارة الأندلس، ومن الكفارات عن ذنوب الناطق
بالضاد، الحج إلى الحمراء التى قال فيها الشاعر :

تمـد لهـا الجـوزاء كف مصافح   ويدنو لها بـدر السماء مناجيا

ومن حظى أنى كنت من الحاجين، زرت البلاد المباركة، وتنشقت هواءها،
وسمعت أهلها يناجون السرور ليل نهار بعيونهم وبأرواحهم الخفيفة، ساعة اللهو
والطرب. ومن غريب الأمور أن فى قلب الأندلس ملجأ قلما يلجأ اليه
الأندلسيون، فهناك مقامٌ لاتُسمع فيه ضجة، ولا تصل إليه أصداء، مقام بل مقامات
هى أجمل ما فى الأندلس أَثرا وذكرا، وقد كان لها من السرور أيام زاهرة، ومن
الطرب ليال باهرة عاطرة، ومن المجد أعلام وقباب، ومعاهد وأنصاب (أعلام
منصوبة)، ما تبقى منها اليوم غير طلول (ما تبقى من آثار) متهدمة نبتت فى
جدرانها الأعشاب، ونظم العنكبوت مرثاته فوق النوافذ منها والأبواب، وجلس
فى عروشها العالية السكون، ودفن فى جناتها المهجورة الشعر والأدب
والفنون... طلول كانت بالأمس معاهدَ وقصورا هى دائرة المجد وقطبُ الحبور
(السعادة والبهجة)، فى قناطرها وقبابها وأبوابها، صناعة نادرة دقيقة وفى كل
رسم من رسومها آية جمال تُدهش حتى اليوم أرباب الفن، وفى كل بيت من
الشعر على جدرانها درة من المعنى أو زهرة من التقوى منقوشة فى بلاط منقطع
النظير، لونا وتذهيبا. هذى آثار العرب، وقد أمست عروشا للنسيان، ومدفنا
لمجد الآباء والأجداد، وظلالا تجلب الأحزان، وعبرة بليغة للانسان، وهى رغم
ذلك بهجة للناظرين، ومصدر وحى للشعراء والمتفننين.

ولكن الذكرى... لله من ذكرى تقبض على النفس فتجعلها كالجماد، لله من
ذكريات وآثار تبتهج لمرآها العين، فيذوب لمعناها الفؤاد !! لله من مجدكم

وعزكم ابن أمية وابن عباد وعبد الرحمن والمنصور والمعتمد من شادوا معاهد العلم والدين...طالما اهتزت النفس لذكر مآثركم، وطالما وقفت العين شفقا عند أسمائكم فى التاريخ.

وتركت ما فى أشبيلية من آثار وذكريات، لأصل غرناطة قاعدة الدنيا فى ذلك الزمان، وحاضرةَ السلطان، ومنها إلى قرطبة مسقط رأس أبى الوليد ابن رشد، لأشاهد الجامع الكبير الذى أصبح كنيسة قائمة على عمد الجامع القديم، ولأدخلَ بيوتا فى المدينة، لم تزل الروح العربية حية فيها، الروح الحافلة بمصابيح من العلم والأدب والفن والشعر كابن رشد، وابن زيدون، والإدريسى، وابن العوام، والخلف أبى القاسم وابن الخطيب، وأصحاب الموشحات...إن مُلكاً شيدوه أمسى أثراً من الآثار، ومجدا أقاموه استحال طللا من الأطلال، ومعاهد علم اسسوها لم يبق منها حجر على حجر، وطفتُ كالهائم الولهان من برج إلى متحف إلى قصر، ووقفت طويلا امام المئذنة التى شادها المهندس العربى جابر للخليفة يوسف بن يعقوب، فانكشفت تحت عينى مدينة هى مشرقية بل مغربية فى سقوفها البيضاء، وجادتها (طرقها) العوجاء، ومصاطبها الحافلة بألوان الأزاهير. وحولت نظرى إلى القصر، وبستانه الفسيح الجميل، ثم إلى برج الذهب الذى بناه ابن العلاء على ضفتى النهر الكبير، فساح بى الفكرُ وجالت بى الأحلام، فأدنتنى من مجد العرب الغابر، بل مثلته أمامى حيا...وتساءلت فى حيرة وألم...ما السبب يا ترى فى سقوط ذلك الملك الذى شعت أنوارُه فى ظلمات أوروبا يوما كنجوم البادية فى الدجى...؟؟ ما السبب فى اضمحلال أركانه وأصوله وقصر عهده وزوال مجده....؟؟

وأقول لن أجيب (الواقع ان الكاتب عالج الأسباب بتوسع لايصلح المقام)...فكتب التاريخ فيها الكثير والعجيب، ولكنى أدعو العرب كل العرب، ليشاهدوا مأ شاهدت فى الأندلس، ليأخذوا العبرة من الآثار والأطلال، فيدركوا أسباب سقوطهم، فيتقوها، حتى لا تفجع الأجيال القادمة بأندلس جديدة (يقصد بفلسطين العربية)، يضيع مع ضياعها بقايا مجدنا وبريق مستقبلنا .

الاستاذ على البهلوان   الثقافة العربية بين الشرق والغرب

الثقافة كالنهر الجارى، ينبوعها الحياة، ومروجها العقل، ومغذيها المجتمع، تكون صافيةً نقيةً طالما نبعت من بيئتها ولم تأخذ من غيرها إلا القدر اليسير، وكذلك كانت الثقافة العربية فى الجاهلية وصدر الاسلام ثقافة كاملة تغلب عليها البداوة، نفسها قصير قوى، سليمة حية، أصولها ثابتة واضحة، وميزاتها بينة جلية، الطبع قوامها وعمادها وأعظمُ خصلة فيها، فقد نبذت الكلفة نبذا، وابتعدت عن التصنع والزخرف. تدفقت الثقافة العربية من عين ثرّة ماؤها صاف غزير، وسرعان ما اتسع النهر المتولد عنها اثر الفتوحات الإسلامية »وأخذت الجداول والأنهار الكبيرة تصبُّ فيها صبا حاملة معها تراث الشعوب ومدنيات الأمم الغابرة والثقافات السابقة....والأعجب أن النهر العربى اقتبل تلك الثروات الطائلة من غير أن ينحرف عن مجراه أو يبدل جوهره وطبعه، بل وهبها من روحه ما امتزجت به وامتزج بها، فخرجت الثقافة الكاملة. الثقافة العربية الإسلامية.

وأخذت الثقافات تدخل العربية عن طريق الترجمة وعن طريق الشعوب التى اسلمت. وعن طريق التبادل التجارى أيضا، فنقلوا فلسفة اليونان وعلومها. وحكمة الهند وتفكيرها، وآداب فارس وحضارتها، فتراكمت لديهم المعلومات، وتشعبت المعارف والفنون، وتعددت طرق البحث والتنقيب...واختلطت السبل فى أول الأمر، وتعكر ماء النهر الصافى، وصعب هضم ذلك الغذاء لتنوعه وكثرته، ولكن النفس العربية لا تعيش إلا فى الوضوح، ولا تزدهر إلا مع البيان، تغلبت على الغموض فخلّصت الأصولَ من الفروع المشتبكة، وأخذ كل علم استقلاله فى موضوعه وطرق البحث الصالحة به، فتجلى شيئا فشيئا ما بين العلوم من ارتباط، وفُتحت آفاق جديدة، وأحدثت علوم لم تكن، كالجبر وعلم المجتمع.

وبذلك كانت الثقافة العربية أحسنَ مثال للثقافة البشرية الكاملة، لأنها ثقافة إنسانية يشملها ضربٌ من الوحدة وإن اتسعت رقعتُها، ولم يكن تنوعها وتشعبها وغزارة موادها وكثرة ابتكاراتها، من عوامل التفرقة بينها والتباين بين المثقفين فى مختلف أقطارها، بل زادها كل ذلك غنى وثروة، وخلق فيها تيارات فكرية ودينية وفنية تربط بين المجتمع وتقرب بين الأفراد.

والثقافة العربية فى العصر الحديث، تسعى جاهدةً للتخلص مما ألصقته بها القرون من أدران، وكبلتها (قيدتها) به من أشكال وقوالب فارقتها الحياة منذ أجيال، فقد مدت يدها إلى تراثها البشرى الكبير وأخذت تزيح عنه النقاب، وتنشر كنوزه متعجبة من تراثه، مكتشفة خفاياه، مستغربة من التماثل (إشارة إلى اثر العرب فى الثقافة الغربية) بينه وبين المدنية الغربية الحاضرة.. ومدت اليد الأخرى إلى الثقافة الغربية تكشف عن غناها وجمالها، وتغترف من علمها الغزير ومحدثاتها المتجددة، وعلينا ألا نخاف من الثقافة ومن الإقبال عليها، فالثقافة الغربية أو الشرقية ضرورية لنا، فستكون كاللقاح تُجدَّدُ به الأشجار فتأتى بأطيب الثمرات، وهى اقاحُ العقل والذوق، وأكبر ميزة لهذه الثقافة اهتمامها بالعلوم الرياضية وتطبيقُها وما أنتجته من اختراعات تطبيقية قامت عليها نهضة الغرب والشرق، فعنايتنا بها يجب أن تحتل المكان الأول من تفكيرنا إذا أردنا الالتحاق بقافلة الأمم الراقية، وليس فى ذلك ما ينافى ثقافتنا، بل إن ذلك سيعززها ويركزها على أسس ثابتة...والثقافة لا تعترف بالحدود فهى ملك الإنسانية عامة، والثقافة تسييرُ نحو الوحدة بخطى سريعة فقد امتزجت المدنياتُ ببعضها واقتربت المسافاتُ بينها وأصبح تبادل المعلومات والخبرات من مميزات عصرنا الحاضر....

ولقد أصبح من المتفق عليه بين مثقفى الوطن العربى أن الثقافة العربية ليست بعض المعلومات اللغوية والبيانية، بل الثقافة العربية كلٌ حىٌ يشمل تاريخا يربط أجزاءها، ومذاهب فلسفية ودينية، وعلوما تولدتْ عنها العلوم العصرية، وشعرا ونثرا عبّرا عن الإنسان فى قوالب فنية تُهذّبُ الذوقَ والعقل...فتدريس الثقافة العربية يتطلب جهودا مستمرة لأن البحثَ العلمى والتمحيص الفكرى لم يشملا إلا القليل منها، فهى ما زالت كالبحر الواسع العميق الذى لم يُعرَفْ منه إلا سواحلُه، فعلينا أن نخوضَ غماره (المياه الكثيرة) وأن نصل قدر المستطاع إلى أعماقه، وعلينا أن نُبعد عن ثقافتنا كل ما يُفسد الذوقَ ويُدخلُ على العقل الغموضَ والاعوجاج، ويُخرج الإنسانَ عن طبعه وجبلته، حتى نضمن لها الصلة بالحياة فلا يقترب منها الذبول، ولا يتسرب إليها الجمود ويكتنفها التكلف والصنعة. فالثقافة الأصيلة تزيد العقل صقلا ونصوعا، والمثقف ليس من يُتقن علما من العلوم حتى يصير مرجعا فيه، بل العلوم هنا تصبح وسيلة لا غاية، إذ غايةُ الغايات الإنسان نفسه، الإنسان بعقله وعواطفه وذوقه وإرادته...فإذا فهمنا ذلك وأدركناه أمكننا أن نلعب دورا خالدا فى العالم كله، وأمكننا أن نعيدَ لثقافتنا مركزها القوى الثرى الذى ضاع بين السلبية والجمود والاتكالية والتخلف.

LESSON THIRTYFIVE

طه حسين محبوبة وشعبان

كانت محبوبة هذه امرأة نصفا (من كان متوسط العمر) تطوف بأهل القرية وتصنع لهم الخبز، وتصنع لهم من الخبز نوعا خاصا هو الذى يُتَّخذُ من الذرة رقيقا مستديرا واهعا، لا تحسن أن تصنع غيره من خبز القمح. فكنتَ تراها فى آخر الليل ملمة (زارها زيارة غير طويلة) بهذه الدار أو بتلك، تهيء العجين. وكنتَ تراها فى أول النهار جالسة أمام الفرن، تدير بيديها السريعة الصَّناع قطع العجين. فتُسويها فى سرعة مدهشة على الشكل الذى ينبغى أن تُسَّوَى عليه ثم تقذفها إلى النار قذفا خفيفا رفيقا. ثم تستردُّها من النار، وقد منحتها النُّضج الذى يجعلها سائغة فى الافواه والحلوق والبطون. وكنت تراها حين يرتفع الضحى عائدة إلى بيتها، وقد حملت أجرها طائفة من هذا الخبز تضيفها إلى طائفة، وتعيش عليها مع زوجها وبنيها وبناتها يقنعون بهذا الخبز فى كثير من الايام. وقد يضيفون إليه هذا الإدام (ما يجعل من الخبز فيطيبه) أو إن ساق الله إلى شعبان رزقا..

وكان شعبان رجلا مقترا عليه (مضيقا عليه فى النفقة) فى الرزق، قد ورث عن ابيه مهنة لا تغنى من جوع. كان بناء متواضعا لا يقيم الدُّور التى تتخذ من الحجر والآجر واللبن، وإنما التى تتخذ من الطين الغليظ : تُراب يُجمع ويُصب عليه الماء ويخلط به بعض الهشيم، ثم تسوى منه قطع متلائمة أو غير متلائمة، يضاف بعضها إلى بعض لتمتد فى الفضاء، وترتفع فى الجو، وتدور أو تستطيل حول رقعة ضيقة من الارض، حتى إذا ارتفعت فبلغت القامة أو أقل، مُد عليها شىء من سعف النخل (قضبانه)، فاستقام منها بيت (نهض واعتدل) أو حُجرة

يأوى إليها البائسون، فتقيمهم أيسر ما ينبغى أن يتقوا من عاديات (العوائق) الطبيعة .

فكان يعمل اليوم أو اليومين ليظل بعد ذلك متعطلا أياما أو اسابيع . وكان يوسع على أهله بهذه القروش التى يُغلُّها : يكسوهم إن استطاع، ويمتعهم بقليل من الطيبات إن طالت يده إلى قليل من الطيبات.

وكانت خديجة ابنتهما كاعما (الفتاة الناهدة) تعمل فى دار من دُور الأغنياء . تُقبل مع الصبح المسفر فتنفق ما تملك من نشاط فى خدمة أهل الدار؛ وتعود مع الليل المظلم إلى بيت أبويها فتنفق الليل فيه . وكانت راضية بهذه الحياة باسمة لها، على شئ من حزن كان يستقر فى قلبها ولا يبين عنه لسانها . كانت تفكر فى بؤس أبويها وإخوتها الصغار، ولكنها لم تكن تعبر عن هذه الخواطر الكئيبة البائسة بلفظ أو لحظ أو حركة، إنما كانت تُخفى حزنها كما يخفى البخيل كنزه، وربما نمت بهذا الحزن نغمة ضئيلة تغمر هذا الصوت الممتلئ العذب، فتترك فى نفوس السامعين اثرا غريبا . كانت حياتها فى تلك الدار بهجة متصلة ورضا مقيما، تقطعهما بين حين وحين فى لحظات قصار هذه النميمة...

معنى الإستقلال   عبد الخالق الطريس

الاستقلال ضرورة، فلذلك نهتف به، ونطلبه، ونستعجل الحصول عليه.

وإن ثمن الاستقلال باهظ (ثقيل)، ولكنه هيّن يسير فى نظر جميع من ذاق مرارة العبودية، وسئم حياة الذل، وفهم معنى الاستقلال، وخيرات الاستقلال، وما يجنيه من الاستقلال.

معنى الاستقلال ـ أيها المواطن ـ أن يكون لك وطن موفور السيادة، ومقام محفوظ فى حظيرة الدول (مجتمع الدول)، وحكومة منك وإليك تَخدِمُ مصلحتك، وتتصرف بإرادتك، وجيش يحميك فى السّلم والحرب، وأسطول يمخر اليم (يشق البحر محدثا صوتا)، ليدفع عنك عوادى النائبات (المصيبة)، ويحمل منك وإليك ما تحتاج إلى تصديره أو توريده، وأجنحة تطير، حاملة اسم بلادك وشعارها لتربطك بالدنيا !

معنى الإستقلال ـ أيها المواطن ـ أن يحكم الشعب نفسه، ويُشرِّعَ لنفسه، ويصون حقوقه ومصالحه بنفسه.

ومعنى الاستقلال ـ ايها المواطن ـ ألّا يعرقل لك تطور، ولا يفرض عليك اتجاه غريب، ولا تساق فى الحروب التى لا مصلحة لك فيها سوق الانعام (البهائم)، ولا تُعطَّل لك قوة، ولا يشرع تشريع تكون أنت أول ضحاياه !

معنى الاستقلال أن تكون حقوق الإنسان كلها محترمة فى وسطك (البيئة)، وأن تكون العدالة التى تحميك من الاعْتِداءِ عدالة نزيهة منظمة، لاتصل إليها أيدى الجهال، ولا يُؤثِّر فيها أى نفوذ غريب عنها !

معنى الاستقلال أن يُقَدَّرُ القَدْرُ الادنى لعيش المواطن، رجلا كان أو أنثى،

حتى لا يضيع أحد بسبب الفقر أو البِطالَةِ أو المرض، وأن يحصل المواطن على حقه فى المسكن والخبز والتَّعلُّم والعلاج...

معنى الاستقلال أن ترى فى بلادك الكفاية من المدارس والكليات والجامعات ومعاهد البحث، والمكاتب والمختبرات والمستشفيات، والمصحات والملاجىء والاصلاحيّات، والمعامل والمصانع، وكلها لك ولفائدتك ورفاهيتك!

معنى الاستقلال أن تكون مدنك مظهرا رائعا من مظاهر المدنية فى المحافظة على الصحة والنظافة وسائر مظاهر التنظيم المدنى، وأن تكون قراك قرى صحية نظيفة تحتوى على كل ما تحتوى عليه القرية فى الامم الراقية، وترتبط فيما بينها بشبكة من المواصلات، وأن تُسَيَّرَ أمور المدينة والقرية بمجالس مُنتخَبةٍ تسهر على راحة السكان ورفاهيتهم!

معنى الاستقلال أن تُنظَّمَ أرضك، وتُدرَسَ دراسة علمية، وأن يُستَغَلُّ كل شبر فيها استغلالا فنيا لتنفع فيما تصلح له، وأن تُستَغَلُّ كل قطرة ماء من مياه أرضك بإنشاء مراكز التوليد الكهربائى والخزانات الكافية، وتنفيذ مشاريع الرَّىِّ لاحياء الارض الموات، وتوليد الارض النَّزُور (الارض القليلة العطاء)، وأن يُستَخْرَجَ ما فى بطن الارض من معادن لتحريك آلة صناعتك، وإيجاد العمل لأمثالك، وتَصْنِيع كل ما فى الميسور من موادها الخام، ليقل الوسطاء، وتنزل بذلك الاسعار!

معنى الاستقلال أن يكون لك نظام مالى بُحكَمٌ، وأساليب اقتصادية مُوَفَّقَةٌ، وأن يكون لأبناء جِلْدَتِكَ وفر، وأن يعظم الدخل القومى، ويرتفع المستوى المعاشى، وأن تكون نسبة التصدير إلى التوريد نسبة معقولة، وأن تكون الميزانية وطنية بكل معانى الكلمة، وُضِعَتْ للمواطنين، لصالحهم، وصالح بلادهم قبل كل شي!

الاستقلال وسيلة قبل أن يكون غاية ؛ فلذلك لايمكن أن يُعَدَّ حلقة نهائية فى سلسلة التطور ؛ إنه الحلقة الاولى . والإصلاح الحقيقى لايأتى إلا بعد الاستقلال . ولا خير فى إصلاح لايأتى على يد أبناء البلاد .

رَأَيْتُكَ رَبِّـــــي ...

عبد الله يوسف احمد

رأيتك ربى خلال النجوم	خلال الضياء خلال القمر
رأيتك ربى خلال الظلام	خلال السحاب خلال المطر
رأيتك ربى خلال الدخان	خلال اللهيب خلال الشرر
خلال السكون خلال الشجون	خلال الغصون خلال الثمر

الهى رأيتك فى الشامخات	وفى الغاب والتل والجدول
وفى النهر يجرى بغير انتهاء	وفى الطفل مذ عامه الاول
وفى الليل يجرى وراء النهار	وفى العشب والريح والشمأل
وكل الخلايا خلايا الحياة	وفى الصمت والكوكب الآفل

رأيتك فى صورة الكائنات	تجسدت ياربُّ هذا الوجود
وسار بأمرك خطو الحياة	ونيدا لدى كل صبح جديد
فهذا زمان أتى مقبلا	وذاك زمان مضى لن يعود
فحق لوجهك أنت الخضوع	وحق علينا دوام السجود

يشب الفطيم بهذا الوجود	بقلب أساريره صافيه
ويأتى الشباب بأحلامه	ويمتلئ الجسم بالعافيه
ويأتى المشيب بأحزانه	يكدّر أيامه الباقيه
ويمضى الهناء ويأتى الفناء	فنعنو لأحكامه القاسيه

وهذا الزمان يثور علينا	فينصفنا تارة أو يجور
وأعمارنا بين أيامه	كقمح عليه الرحايا تدور
فنذهب من صخب هذى الحياة	لتحضننا صامتات القبور
هى الأم تحضن كل الورى	وذا دأبها من قديم العصور

فكم أخرس الدهر شحرورة   تغنت زمانا على الرابيه

وكم أذبل الدهر روضا نضيراً   فأمست فراشاته باكيه

وكم جفف الدهر ماء الغدير   وماء الينابيع والساقيه

وكم أمة بعد أخرى مضت   وكم أمم بعدها آتيه

هو الدهر نحن على دربه   نسير كما سارت القافله

ونمضى كطيف وراء الشعاع   كما تفعل الانجم الآفله

كأنشودة البلبل الحر يشدو   وقد أسكتته يد قاتله

كمر الرياح كنور الصباح   كذوب الشدى كالرؤى العاجله

الزنبقـة العـاشـقـة

الدكتور عيسى درويش

وأرتنى ثغرها العذب الجميـل	بسمت زنبقـة لى مـرة
من فتى أصبح كالعود نحيـل»	قلت : «يازنبقـتى ما المبتغى
وبدمع من مآقيها .. يسيـل	فأجابتنى بصوت ناعـم
ان فى حبك مـا يشفى العليـل	إن يكن جسمك مـن داء ذوى
أى نفع فى هوانا المستحيـل	قلت: «يازنبقـة الروض اشمعى
هـل لانسـان عن الموت بـديـل	فى غد يسقطنـا الموت بـه
يستوى فيه كثير وقليـل	يسقط العمـر على ابوابه
وكلانا بين جنبيـه قتيـل	قلمـا نرشف مـن كأس الهوى
جاء يرتاح على الغصـن الخضيـل	صاح بالزنبق طير عاشـق
ولكم جئت الى هـذا الخميـل	«آه يا أختـاه انى عـاشـق
ربما ألقى لمن أهوى سبيل	أرقب الآفـاق أرضـا وسمـا
فاذا راح الهـوى ـ آن الرحيـل»	إنمـا الأيـام حب دائـم
الشـذى .. والشعر والحب الأصيـل	قلت: «ياطير الهوى طاب اللقـا
هات يازنبقـتى ـ روى الغليـل	أعطنـى اللحن وخذ أغنيـتى
وامزج العطر بهـذا السلسبيـل	واجعـل العمر ربيعـا دائـما
عدت مزهـوا مـع الصبح البليـل»	فاذا غبت. على لـوح الدجى
حلت الأحزان والهم الثقيـل	يا أخى الانسـان لاتيأس اذا
شاءها الله فما ضيق يـطوﻝ	واجعل الايام تمسى مثلمـا
واختـم النعمة بالشكر الجزيـﻞ	وعش اللحظـة فى نشوتها
ودع الشر مـن الدنيا يـزوﻝ	واطلب الخيـر الس كل الورى

غُبـار .. غُبـار !

خليـل الهنـداوى

فليـس على الـدرب إلا الغبـار   ركَضُنا ، بَرَى الركضُ أقدامنا

ويدفعنـا السّيـل عَبـرَ القِفـار   نروح ونغدو ، نكدُّ ونشقى

كما يـذبل الـزهر بعـد ازهـار   ونطَوى ، وتذبلُ آمالُنـا

بُعيـد النَّـوى تحتوينا الديـار !   نشيد الديـار ، وياليتنـا

لنبقى ، فتضحك منا الحجار !   ونُعلى الحجارة فوق الـرفـات

نـريد الفـرار ، وأيـن الـفـرار ؟   ونركض فى الليـل ، عبر النهار

وعمـا قـريب يُخَطُّ السِتـار   لمـاذا أتينـا؟ ومـاذا جنينـا؟

هـو الحلمُ ، رفَّ جنـاحـا، وطـار   وتغتمض العين عن عـالـم

وبعـد غـد ، لا سـؤال يُثـار   غـدا ، سـوف يكثـرُ عنا السـؤالُ

ويسطـع للمُدلجيـن النهـار   وقد تشرق الشمس مـن بعدنا

ولم نُفـرّع الـروضَ بعـد اخضرار   كأن لم نجئ سـاعةً للحيـاة

وحولك أوراقهـا فـى نثـار   ويا عابرا بيديك الزهـور

تطُـوع عبيـرا، وتزهو احمـرار !   كأن دماءك فـى وردهـا

فأنت ، مسـاءً ، طعـامُ الغَرار   تمتَّـع صباحـا بشم القـرارِ

بمـاذا تشك ؟ لمـاذا تحـار ؟   هـو العقل أعطـاك حكمَ اليقيـن

تطـول الليـالى ، وهنَّ القِصار   تمسكت بالعيش ، تبغى الخلـود

وركـابها أبـدا فـى انتظـار   تمر الحيـاة مـرورَ القطـار

ولاشئ .. لا شئ إلا الغُبـار   قـوافل يعدو عليهـا الفنـاء

LESSON FORTY

المجـذوب

عمر ابو قوس

ما كان مجنونـا وان سخـروا بـه — لكـن يرى مـا لا يَرونَ ويسمـعُ

ساهى الجفـون كأنمـا نظراتـه — شـدَّت الى نـور بعيـد يلمـعُ

أبصرئه فى السـوق يخطب نرة — والنـاس مـن احوالـه تجمـع

هيا أعشقـوا مثلى وغنوا حبكم — وتـزودوا مـن دهركم وتمتعـوا

فالحب ريحـان الحيـاة وروحـها — وضيـاؤها واريجهـا المتضوع

وأنـا المحب المستـهـام بفاتـنٍ — ملأ الوجـود جمالـه المتنوع

ضاقت به الدنيـا ورحب فضائها — ونجـومها وحنت عليـه الأضلـع

ولقد أناجيه فاسمـع صوتـه — واحسـه فى مهجتييتربع

هامت بـه الافلاك فـى عليائهـا — والهـاتفـات على الغصون السّجُع

والبرق والرعـد المـدَوى والحيـا — والـزهـر والـروض الجميـل الممرع

كلّ يسبح بـاسمـه متشوقـا — لوصالـه وهو العزيـز الأمنـع

حتى الحجـارة تغتليذراتهـا — شـوقـا اليـه ققلبهـا متصدّع

دارت عـلى أقـطـابـهـن رواقصاً — طربـا على نغـمٍ لهـنَ يوقّ

مهى الدراويش الصغـار فديتها — بالهـاجعين وليلهـا لا يهجـع

سكت الخطيب وأدركته حسـرة — كادت لها أحشـاؤه تتقطـع

فتضاحك النظار مـن أقـوالـه — ورثـوا لـه مـن رحمـة وتوجعوا

ومضى وفى يُمنَى يـديـه هراوة — يزوِى بها الصبيان عنه ويـردع

LESSON FORTYONE

نشيــد افريقيــة

محمـد الفيتـورى

يا أخى فى الشَّرقِ فى كُلِّ سَكَنْ	يا أخى فى الأرضِ فى كُلِّ وطَنْ
أنا أدْعوكَ فَهَل تَعرِفُنى	يا أخاً أعرِفُهُ رَغمَ المِحَنْ
إننى مَزَّقْتُ أكْفانَ الدُّجَى	إننى هَدَمْتُ جُدرانَ الوَهَنْ
لم أعُدْ مَقْبَرَةً تَحكِى البِلى	لم أعُد ساقيةً تَبْكى الدِّمَنْ
أنا حىٌّ خالدٌ رغم الرَّدَى	أنا حُرٌّ رَغمَ قُضبانِ الزَّمَنْ

إن نَكُن سِرنا على الشَّوكِ سِنينا	ولَقينا مِن أذاهُ ما لَقينا
إن نَكُن بِتنا عُراةً جائِعينا	أو نَكُن عِشنا حُفاةً بائسينا
إن نَكُن أوهنت الفَأسُ قُوانا	وَقَفْنا نَتحَدَّى الظّالمينا
إن نَكُن سَخَّرنا جَلّادُنا	فَبَنينا لأمانينا سُجونا
فَلَقَد ثُرنا على أنفُسِنا	و مَحونا وصَمَة الذِّلَّة فينا

المَلايينُ أفاقَت مِن كَراها	ما ثراها مَلأَ الأُفقَ صَداها؟
خَرجَت تَبْحَثُ عَن تاريخِها	بعدَ أن تاهَت على الأرضِ وتاها
حَمَلَت أنؤُسَها وانحَدَرت	من رَوابيها وأغوارِ ثُراها
فانظُرِ الإصرارَ فى أعيُنِها	وصياحَ البَعثِ يَجتاحُ الجِباهْ
يا أخى فى كُلِّ أرضٍ وَجَمَت	شَفَتاها واكفَهَرَّت مُقلَتاها
قُم تَحَرَّر مِن ثَوابِتِ الأسَى	لَسْتَ أُعْجُوبَتَها أو مُوميْاها
إنطَلِق فَوقَ ضُحاها ومَساها	يا أخى قَد أصبَحَ الشَّغبُ إلها

الخبــر

صلاح عبد الصبور

يلقى بى ضجرى أحيانا فى شط البحـر
يستهوينى عندئذ أن أهمس للموج المتدفق
بأفانين القصص المنحولة عن نفسى
أو اعلن عن اسمائى فى ابواق الافق المطبق
فاسمى نفسى احيانا بالقرصان الازرق
او بالتنيـن المحـرق   ****

احيـانا تلقى بى الاسفـار الى الغابـات
فى وحشتها تستيقظ فى نفسى التهـويمات
ويغمغم صـوتى بالكلمـات المدخـولات
واقـدم نفسى للشجر الملتف
باسم : الاعـصار العاصف   ****

فى هـاوية الجبـل المسنون اسمى نفسى بالسيل القاصف
فى صخر السفـح الغافى فى جدران الصمت
اسمى نفسى :
قطب الـوقت   ****

مـن يدرينى اذ يهـبط ظلى فى ظلى
حيـن اعود الى ظلمـة بيتى
بـم تفتـر ثنـايـا الـزبد البيضـاء
وبمـاذا تصفـر سـاخـرة اشجار الغابـات
مـاذا بث الجبل المتوحد للجبل المتوحد عـن هـازل احوالى
فى مـرتحلى أو فى حلى
مـن غمـزات او ايمـاءات
مـاذا غمغـم فى قيعـان السفـح الغافـى
مـن سخـريـة الاصـوات   ****

آه .. ضقت بحـالى ، بأكـاذيبى ضـقت
لـو يلتف على عنقى احد الحبـلين
الـصدق ...
او الـصمـت .

إذا

قصيـدة روديارد كبلنـج الخالـدة
ترجمة : الدكتور صفاء خلـوصى

اذا استطعت ان تحتفظ برأسك عندما يفقد كل من حواليك

رؤوسهم وينحون عليك باللائمة

اذا وثقت بنفسك عندما يفقد كل انسان ثقته فيك،

وتترك مع ذلك مجالا للشك،

اذا استطعت ان تنتظر دون ان تمل الانتظار

او أن يعاملك الآخرون بالكذب من دون ان تلجأ اليه

او تكون موضع كراهية، ولكنك لا تدع لها مجالا للتسرب الى نفسك

ولا تبدو أفضل مما ينبغى، ولا تتكلم بحكمة اكثر مما يجب.

اذا استطعت ان تحلم، ولا تدع للأحلام سيادة عليك،

اذا استطعت ان تفكر، ولا تجعل الافكار غايتك القصوى،

اذا استطعت ان تجابه الفوز والفشـل

وتعامل هذين المخاتلين الخادعين على حـد سواء،

اذا استطعت ان تكدس كل ما تملك من ارباح

وتغامر بها دفعة واحـدة

وتخسرها جميعا ثم تبدأ من جـديد،

من دون ان تنطق بكلمة واحدة عن خسارتك،

اذا استطعت ان تخاطب الجماهير من غير ان تتخلى عن فضائلك،

وان تسير فى ركاب الملوك من دون ان تفقد مزاياك المعتادة،

اذا عجز الاعداء والاصدقاء والمحبون عن اثارة حفيظتك بايذائهم اياك،

اذا كان الناس كلهم عندك سواسية، من دون ان يكون لأى منهم اهمية خاصة

اذا استطعت ان تملأ الدقيقة الغاضبة التى لاتغفر لأحد

بما يعادل ستين ثانية من السعى ركضا،

فلك الارض وما عليها،

وأنت، فوق ذلك كله، ستكون رجلا، يابنى!!..

نهــاية حب

الحبيب شيبوب

تناسيتِ العهودَ، وخُنت حبى   ولم تترقّى أبدا بقلبى

وأغراك السرابُ فطرت نَشوَى   لآفاق السراب ، بغير لب

وكنت أخال قلبك ـ ان دعاه   سوى داعى حبيبك ـ لايلبى

فمالك والحنين الى سواه   كأنك لم تكونى ـ امس ـ قربى

ولم تُشرِق بلقيانا عَشايا   طويناها على أمل وحب

فما صرف الفؤادَ نذيرِ شكّ   ولا عصفت به نزوَات عَتب

وكان الوكر حنتنا ، وكنا   به طفلين فى نزق ولعب

تحجبنا ستائره فنلهو   ونشرب للغرام الـذ نخب

وولّى هكذا عامان كانا   كحلم، فى ليالى الصيف، عـذب

فكنت وفية حينا ، وحينا   أراك على مواربة وكذب

فلم اكتمك ما قد حدثتنى   به نفسى . ولم يك رجم غيب!

فأنكرت الهواجس من ظنونى   وقلت بان ذلك محض ريب

ولم أحفل بما زعموا ، الى ان   رأيتكما معا جنبا لجنب

رأيتكما ، فما صدقت عينى   وخانتنى قواى ، وضاق رحبى

اذا انسدل الظلام يطول سهدى   وان طلع الصباح يضل ركبى

فقد بلغت حكايتنا مداها   وقد كشف المخبأ والمخبى

وها قد جئت ما ارسلت دمعا   ولا أقررت ، شاعرة بـذنب

فكيف تؤملين لدى صفحا   وكيف وسهمك الدامى بجنبى

فعودى غير آسفة اليـه   ولاتخشنى ـ وإن أفضعك ـ حربى

وتيهى فى ضلالك ، واحتسيها   كؤوسَ ندامة ، بمرير شـرب

وكونى مثلما تبغين. لكـن   اعيذك من مفاجأة المهـب

وما قد فات ، ليس يعود يوما   وجرحى غير مندمل بطب

إليك، إليك، لست فتى لعوبا   ولستُ الى سواك بمشـرب

وحسبك من غرامى ذكريات   فنهرى ليس يرجع للمصب

The Arabic Writing

IN FIVE LESSONS

with Practical Exercises and a Key

by F. E. Sommer

Preface

THE ARABIC LETTERS are used over an immense area, from Morocco to Chinese Turkestan, for writing not only all the Arabic dialects but also other languages of importance, such as Hindustani, Persian and Malay. The ability to read the Arabic writing, therefore, is a valuable key to the Near East.

Most text books simply give a table of the letters with their different forms, leaving it to the student to memorize them. In this pamphlet the study of the writing is separated from that of the language and the student is gradually introduced to the intricacies of the Arabic graphic system.

Those who are willing to put in a few weeks of study should feel well rewarded when they can make out names on signs, labels or maps and read separate words or even short sentences. A knowledge of the Arabic letters also provides the necessary basis for the study of any of the languages using them.

The Author

Lesson I

THE ARABIC WRITING is very graceful and decorative. The letters are of such a flexible shape that they can be dilated to fill the line because the practice of breaking up words is banned in Arabic texts. Leaving aside the abbreviated style of rapid cursive writing, we shall consider only the common printed form called NASKHI which is used also in careful handwriting.

The Arabic letters are written *from right to left.* Several groups of letters are derived from the same basic forms, the various letters being distinguished by the number and the position of the accompanying dots. We begin with the basic form ب from which 3 consonants are derived:

بـ B   تـ T   ثـ Th

(The tie indicates that two letters represent *one* Arabic character.)

These sounds are easily memorized if we remember that *B* has a dot *below, T two* dots on *top,* while *Th* is characterized by *three* dots.

If we make this basic form deeper, almost like a half-circle, and write it in a slightly slanting position with one dot in the middle we get the letter

ن N.

SHORT VOWELS

The three short vowels (a in cat, i in pin and u in put) are indicated by vowel marks placed above or below the *preceding* consonant:

بَ ba   بِ bi   بُ bu.

At the beginning of a word, a special "prop" is used to support the vowel mark. It is a simple vertical line called "alif" and representing the first letter of the Arabic alphabet:

أَ a-   إِ i-   أُ u-.

SUKŪN

In the Arabic conception the vowel marks are no more than reading aids which can be omitted. One might think that in texts with full reading marks the absence of a vowel mark would be a sufficient indication that no vowel is to be read. But there is a special mark °, called sukūn or rest, which confirms the absence of a vowel sound.

The form بْ makes it plain that we have to read simple b, not ba, bi or bu. The resemblance of sukūn to zero may help in remembering its function.

FINAL AND INITIAL FORMS

The forms ب ت ث ن are used when these letters stand alone; it is their *detached form*. When con-

nected with the preceding letter at the *end of a word*
they merely add a connecting stroke at the right side.

ﺐ   ﺕ   ﺕ   ﺙ   ﻦ   are *final forms*.

For connection with the following letter, that means
to the left, only the first half of the detached form is used
and the dots are moved to the right; this gives us the
initial forms

ﺑ b-,   ﺗ t-,   ﺛ th-,   ﻧ n-.

Examples: ﺑَﺖْ bat, ﺗِﻦْ tin, ﺛُﺐْ' thub, ﻧِﺚْ nith.

LONG VOWELS

The three symbols used to indicate the long vowels ā,
ī, ū are: ﺍ , which has no sound by itself, ﻭ w and ﻯ y.
The consonants w and y represent vowels only in combination with the vowel marks ُ and ِ .

ā (as in far or bath) ﺑَﺎ ﻧَﺎ ﺗَﺎ ﺛَﺎ bā nā tā thā

ī (as in police, never as i in bite) ﺑِﻰ ﻧِﻰ ﺗِﻰ ﺛِﻰ bī
nī tī thī

ū (as in rule) ﺑُﻮ ﻧُﻮ ﺗُﻮ ﺛُﻮ bū, nū, tū, thū.

The consonant y (ﻯ), which represents long ī, is in
its initial form similar to initial b, but with two dots
below: ﺑ b-, ﻳ y-. The final forms of y and w are so
natural that they need not be discussed: ﻳﻰ or ﻳِﻲ yī,
ﻳُﻮ yū.

USE OF THE INITIAL FORM

Not all the letters can be connected at the left side. ﺍ
and ﻭ are two of the letters which have only a detached

and a final form.   After such letters there is always a gap
because the following consonant appears in its initial
form.   It is just like starting a new word, except for the
spacing.   The term "initial form," consequently, does
not apply only to the beginning of a word.   At the end of
a word, after one of the two-form letters, the detached
form is required because there can be no connection on
either side.

Examples: اِبْتْ ibt — وَتَانْ watān — تُوبَا tūbā —
تَابُوتْ tābūt — نَاثْ nāth — اَوَاتْ awāt (the
last word contains 4 detached forms!).

Exercise 1

(Write with Roman letters, then check with the Key at
the end)

1 بَانِى 2 يُوفُو 3 يَاتِى 4 تُورِنى 5 بُوتْ
6 تَابِتْ 10 يُونَانْ 9 بِنْ 8 نَابْ 7 تَابِى
11 تَارِنى 12 بَابْ .

Lesson II

LONG INITIAL VOWELS

AT THE beginning of a word, the vowel marks which pre-
cede the letters ا, و, ى in long vowel combinations are
supported by the prop alif, just as in the case of short
initial vowels. But instead of اَا only one alif is written

while the second alif assumes the shape of an auxiliary
mark on top, called MADDA (lengthening):

آ ā-, اِي‍ ī- (ee), اُو ū-.

Examples: آب āb — آتُو ātū — آنِي ānī — اُوتَا
ūtā — اِيت īt — اُونِي ūnī — اِين īn.

CONNECTION ON BOTH SIDES

We know that b, t, t͡h, n, y connected with a following
letter have the forms بـ, تـ, ثـ, نـ, يـ. When connected simultaneously with the preceding letter, in other
words at both ends, they assume the following *medial
forms:* ـبـ, ـتـ, ـثـ, ـنـ, ـيـ.

Examples: (From now on, final sukūn will be omitted.
   Its presence is inferred as long as no vowel mark
   is present).

بَنَت banat — نِبُث nibut͡h — ثُبَت t͡hubat —
يَثِنت yat͡hint — بِنت bint (daughter) — اِبْن
ibn (son).

DIPHTHONGS—DOUBLING OF
LETTERS

The letters ى and و represent the long vowel sounds
ī and ū *only* when preceded by the *corresponding* short
vowel mark (ِ or ُ); otherwise they remain the consonants y and w. Examples: اُو ū, اَو aw, اِى ī, اَى ay,
بَيْت nūn, نَوْن nawn, نَوَن nawan, بِيت bīt,
bayt.

The doubling of a letter is not indicated by writing the

letter twice, but by placing over the consonant a special auxiliary mark ّ , called tashdīd or strengthening. Its similarity to our "double U" may remind of its function.

نِتّ nitt,   تَنَّا tannā,   ثُبَّ thubba.

Exercise 2   Transliterate the following words:

1 نُوبَا 2 نُبَا 3 بَنِى 4 بِنُو 5 ثِين 6 اِنْتِنَات

7 اَبَّان 8 آيَات 9 اِينُوت 10 آنَوْت 11 بَابَا

12 آنَا 13 اَنْتَ 14 نَبَات .

Lesson III

LETTERS WITH TWO FORMS ONLY

BESIDE ا and و there are four other letters which cannot be connected with the following letter and which, there-fore, have only two forms: one detached and one con-nected with the preceding letter (final form).

ر ـر R ز ـز Z د ـد D ذ ـذ Dh (voiced th in than)

Examples: رَاد rād – رِينُو rīnū – رُوزِى rūzī – زَارِى zārī – زِرَّا zirrā – زُودَان zūdān – زَوْد zawd – ذِرْزُو dhirzū – دِينَا dīnā.

All other letters have 4 forms: detached, initial, medial and final.

THE BASIC FORM ح

ح Ḥ Strongly aspirated from the breast; no equiva-lent in English.

خ Kh   Scotch or German ch in loch, Buch.   It is commonly transliterated by kh, although this combination misrepresents the actual sound.

ج J   (as in join).   In Syria like French j (s in pleasure); in Egypt g as in go.

When connected, these letters undergo a considerable change of form.   Connection with the following letter: حـ خـ جـ   Connection on both sides: حكـ خـ جـ   Final forms: ح ـع ـج ـخ *Examples:* بَخْت bakht – نَجِيد najīd – حَرَار ḥarār – جُورَا jūrā – رِيح rīḥ (wind) – خَبَر khabar (news) – بُرْج burj (tower) – بَحْر baḥr (sea).

ل L (Lām)

At the end of a word or when standing alone, L has the shape of a hook reaching below the line: ل , ـل . The initial and medial forms stand on the line ل , ـلـ . The combination of ل with ا is not written لا but لا or لا .

The definite article "al," corresponding to English "the," is written together with the noun: اَلْبُرْج al-burj, the tower.

Examples: لَاب lāb – لَجَل lajal – بَلِل balil– اَلْبِلَاد al-bilād.

Exercise 3

آخِر 5 وَلَد 4 لَبَن 3 لُبْنَان 2 اَوَّل 1
نَار 10 دَلِيل 9 حَدِيد 8 بَرِيد 7 جَبَل 6

14 زَوَاج   13 جَوَاب   12 تَلّ   11 دَخَل

15 قَاجِى   16 اَلْوَزِير   .

Lesson IV

THE CHARACTERS for S (as in so) and S͡h (as in she) have the same form, differentiated by three dots.

) ‏مـسـ‎ medial , ‏سـ‎ initial , ‏سى‎ S (final: ‏س‎ ‏سں‎

) " ‏شى‎ , " ‏شـ‎ , " ‏مشـ‎ (S͡h ‏ش‎

We use Q to transcribe a guttural K-sound whose Arabic symbol is similar to that of F (as in fun).

) ‏ـفـ‎ :medial , ‏فـ‎ , initial ‏ـفى‎ F (final: ‏فـ‎ ‏فب‎

) " ‏ـقى‎ , " ‏قـ‎ , " ‏ـقـ‎ (Q ‏ق‎

Note that in the detached and final forms Q has the deep outline of ‏ن‎ while F is flat, like ‏حب‎ .

Examples: ‏سَال‎ sāl, ‏فِسُّور‎ fisūr, ‏سِفَاق‎ sifāq, ‏قَاشُوَار‎ qāshwār, ‏نِيسَان‎ nīsān (April), ‏سَيْفِ‎ sayf (sword), ‏نَقْش‎ naqs͡h (painting), ‏فَرَس‎ faras (horse).

M — K — H

M (as in my; final ‏ع‎ or ‏م‎ , initial ‏مـ‎ , medial ‏ـمـ‎)

K (as in kin; final ‏ـكى‎ or ‏ـلى‎ , initial ‏كـ‎ , medial ‏ـكـ‎). [The upper stroke is written last.]

H (as in he); final ‏ـه‎ , initial ‏هـ‎ , medial ‏ـهـ‎).

When the final or detached form of H at the end of a
word is provided with two dots on top, we get a final letter
characteristic of the feminine gender: ﺓ , ﺔ . Its
classical pronunciation is t, which explains its name "Tā
marbūta" (bound T). Now it has that sound only after
ā (اِمْرَاﺓ imrāt, woman) or when followed by a defining
word; otherwise it is short "a". سِكَّة is read sikka, but
سِكَّة حَدِيد sikkat hadīd (railroad). We transliterate by 't.

H A M Z A (ﻫﻤﺰﺓ)

The sign ﻉ, called hamza, indicates the opening of the
throat, similarly to the Greek ᵓ. It is a slight break or
hiatus which we articulate when we say "the ear" or "co-
operate." At the beginning of a word, hamza always
accompanies the vowel carrier alif although أ, إ, أ are
commonly written for the more correct أَ, إِ, أُ .

Hamza distinguishes the alif at the beginning of a word
or syllable from the lengthening alif, which indicates long
ā. In the word أَوْﻻَد al-awlād, the children, the first
and the second alif are accompanied by hamza, but not
the third alif. This explains why the same combination ﻻ is read differently.

Hamza sometimes appears alone, but most of the time
it is supported by one of the long vowel symbols ا, ﻭ,
ﻱ, depending on the following or preceding vowel.
The rules determining the carrier are too complex to be
given here.

Hamza even can be accompanied by sukūn. It may seem strange that there could be an opening of the throat without vowel sound, but the phonetic effect is that of a slight gap in the pronunciation of the word.

Examples: سَأَلَ sa'ala, he asked; سُئِلَ su'ila, he was asked.

(The dots under the y are omitted in this case.)

In رُؤُوس ru'ūs, heads, the first و serves as a carrier for the hamza, while the second one indicates the long ū sound. Hamza with sukūn occurs in the words رَأْس ra's, head, بِئْر bi'r, water well, بُؤْس bu's, misfortune. In the spoken language this amounts now to a simple lengthening of the vowel (rās, bīr, būs).

Exercise 4 (*To be transliterated*)

كِتَاب 2 يَوْم 3 مَلِك 4 مَمْلَكَة 5 مَكْتُوب 1
كُلّ 7 مَكْتَبَة 8 تَذْكِرَة 9 حَمَّام 10 لَحْم 6
اَلْبَرْق 12 اَلْقَلَم 13 فَهَم 14 كَبِير 15 نَهْر 11
جَزِيرَة 17 شَهْر 18 شَرْق . 16

SOLAR AND LUNAR LETTERS

The definite article ال, written together with a noun, is not always pronounced "al." Before t, tĥ, d, dĥ, r, z, s, ŝh, s̲, d̲, t̲, z̲, l, n (the 14 solar letters) the l is assimilated to the first letter of the noun which, as a result, appears doubled. Al-ŝhams is pronounced aŝh-ŝhams, al-nūr becomes an-nūr, al-raḫīm ar-raḫīm, etc. In writing, this can be indicated by placing the mark of doubling over the first letter of the noun: اَلرَّحِيم، اَلنُّور، اَلشَّمْس .

All other letters are so-called lunar letters and do not affect the article: al-bahr, al-manzil, al-qamar. The words shams, sun, and qamar, moon, have given their name to the group to which their initial letter belongs: sh—solar, q—lunar.

Lesson V

THE remaining consonants can be arranged in groups of two:

DETACHED	FINAL	INITIAL	MEDIAL	SOUND	REMARKS
ص	ص	صـ	ـصـ	S	Formed farther back in the mouth than s.
ض	ض	ضـ	ـضـ	D	Similar to th in thou.
ط	ط	ط	ط	T	The tongue is pressed against the middle of the palate. The vertical stroke is written last.
ظ	ظ	ظ	ظ	Z	Mostly pronounced Z.

ع   ح   ﻊ   ﯖ   ᶜ(ayn) A sudden clos-
ﺍ   ing of the

                              throat, much

                              stronger than

                              hamza.

غ   ﺥ   ﻐ   ﻎ   Ĝh Between r and

                              k͡h. French r

                              grasseyé.

NUNATION

Nunation (Arabic: tanwīn) is the addition of the letter
nūn (N) to a short vowel at the end of a word.   This is
expressed by the doubling of the vowel mark: ⸏ an, ⸰ in,
ᵍ un.

In the literary language the termination ᵍ (-un) plays
the part of the indefinite article, while ⸰ and ⸏ are in-
flectional endings (genitive, accusative); -an also is an
adverbial ending, the only nunation retained in collo-
quial speech.   In the latter case, it is accompanied by
final alif: جِدًّا jiddan, very; أَيْضًا aydan, also;
كِتَابٌ kitābun, a book.

WASL

Another auxiliary mark of the literary language is waṣl
(ﯢ) which indicates that the alif over which it is placed
has lost its sound in favor of the preceding vowel.
فِى ٱلْبَيْت fī 'l-bayt, in the house (instead of fī
al-bayt).

The waṣl could be compared to our apostrophe in contractions such as "you're" for "you are".

VARIANTS

The letters of the form ﺤ can have a preceding consonant superscribed, e.g. ﻒ , ﻞ , ﻤ etc., instead of ﻤﻜ , ﻟﺒﺞ , ﻓﻜﻤ .

ﻄ ﻂ and ﺴﺎ can be written for ﻟﻢ and ﺴﻤﺎ . Final ﺓ is the same as ﻯ . In northern Africa F and Q are designated by ﺒ and ﺪ (instead of ﻒ , ﻖ).

NUMERALS

Although we call our numerals "Arabic," the Arabs use the following figures which are combined from left to right, just like ours:

١	٢	٣	٤	٥	٦	٧	٨	٩	٠
1	2	3	4	5	6	7	8	9	0

1852 is written ١٨٥٢ but this is due to the fact that the Arabs reverse our order of pronouncing the numerals. They read from right to left: two and fifty and eight hundred and a thousand.

Exercise 5 (Transliterate)

1 طَبِيب 2 عِلْم 3 مِصْر 4 سَاعَة 5 طَيِّب
6 غَرْب 7 سُلْطَان 8 عَيْن 9 لَفْظ 10 صَاحِب
11 عَرَبِى 12 لُغَة 13 عَرَف 14 طَرِيق 15
19 مُؤَلِّف 16 اَلشَّجَر 17 شَارِع 18 اَحْمَد
20 مُحَمَّد عَلِى .

ALPHABETICAL ORDER — DICTIONARIES

In the Arabic alphabet the letters are grouped by similarity of form:

ا	alif	د	dāl	ض	ḍād	ك	kāf
ب	bā	ذ	dhāl	ط	ṭā	ل	lām
ت	tā	ر	rā	ظ	zā	م	mīm
ث	thā	ز	zā	ع	'ayn	ن	nūn
ج	jīm	س	sīn	غ	ghayn	و	wāw
ح	ḥā	ش	shīn	ف	fā	ه	hā
خ	khā	ص	ṣād	ق	qāf	ى	yā

In Arabic dictionaries the words are listed under the first letter of the *root*, which is not always the first letter of the word.   But there are now dictionaries in which a reference to the root is given under the first letter of the word.

Exercise 6 (*Write in Arabic letters*)

1 lisān 2 al-ḥaywān 3 al-ism 4 al-madīnaẗ 5 an-nīl 6 insān 7 al-ukht 8 al-kursī 9 dīn 10 firāsh 11 janīnaẗ 12 al-miftāḥ 13 laymūn 14 zahar 15 fallāḥ 16 nazārat 17 afrīqā.

KEY TO THE EXERCISES

(Unless a meaning is given, the word is made up for the sake of practice)

I

1 Bānī 2 būnū 3 yātī 4 tūnī 5 būt 6 tābī 7 nāb 8 yin

9 yūnān 10 t͡hābit (fixed) 11 t͡hānī (the second) 12 bāb (door).

II

1 nūbā 2 nubā 3 banī 4 bitū 5 t͡hīnu 6 intināt 7 abbān·
8 āyāt 9 īnūt 10 anawt 11 bābā 12 anā(I) 13 anta (thou)
14 nabāt (plants).

III

1 awwal (first) 2 lubnān (Lebanon) 3 laban (milk) 4
walad (boy) 5 āk͡hir (the past) 6 jabal (mountain) 7 barīd
(cold) 8 ḥadīd (iron) 9 dalīl (guide) 10 nār (fire) 11 dak͡hal
(to enter) 12 tall, commonly tell, (hill) 13 jawāb (reply)
14 zawāj (marriage) 15 tājir (merchant) 16 al-wazīr (the
vizier).

IV

1 kitāb (book) 2 yawm (day) 3 malk (king) 4 mamlakat͡
(country) 5 maktūb (letter) 6 kull (all) 7 maktabat͡ (office,
bookstore) 8 tad͡hkarat͡ (passport) 9 ḥammām (bath) 10
laḥm (meat) 11 al-barq (the lightning) 12 al-qalam (the
pen) 13 faham (to understand) 14 kabīr (great) 15 nahr
(river) 16 jazīrat͡ (island) 17 s͡hahr (city) 18 s͡harq (east).

V

1 ṭabīb (physician) 2 ᶜilm (science) 3 Miṣr (Egypt) 4
sāᶜat͡(hour) 5 ṭayyib (good) 6 g͡harb (west) 7 sulṭān (sultan)
8 ᶜayn (eye) 9 lafẓ (pronunciation) 10 ṣāḥib (master) 11
ᶜarabī (Arabic) 12 lug͡hat͡ (word) 13 ᶜaraf (to know) 14
ṭarīq (road) 15 muʾallif (author) 16 as͡h-s͡hajar (the tree)
17 s͡hāriᶜ (street) 18 Aḥmad 19 Muḥammad 20 ᶜalī.

VI

اَلْمَدِينَة 4 اَلِأْ سم 3 اَلْحَيْوَان 2 لِسَان 1
اَلْكُرْسِى 8 اَلْأُخْت 7 إِنْسَان 6 اَلنِّيل 5
اَفْرِيقَا 17 نَظَارَة 16 فَلَّاح 15 زَهَر 14 لَيْمُون 13 اَلْمِفْتَاح 12 جَنِينَة 11 فِرَاش 10 دِين 9 .

(*Translation* of the words: 1 tongue 2 the animal 3 the
name 4 the city 5 the Nile 6 man 7 the sister 8 the chair 9
religion 10 bed 11 garden 12 the key 13 lemon 14 flower
15 fellah, farm laborer 16 ministry 17 Africa.)

ADAPTATION OF THE ARABIC WRITING TO OTHER LANGUAGES

To express sounds lacking in Arabic, new symbols are
created by modifying the number and the position of the
dots.

Persian adds the following symbols: پ p, گ g, چ
ch, ژ zh (French j).

Hindustani has, besides: ٹ (or ٿ) ṭ, ڈ ḍ, ڑ ṛ,
ں (nasal sound).

Malay uses غ ṅg, ڤ p, ڽ ñya.

Afghan adds 9 symbols to the Hindustani alphabet for
special sounds which cannot be described here: ڼ , څ ,
ښ , ړ , ږ , ڦ , ڵ , ڋ , گ .

The greatest variety of symbols is found in *Sindhi:*

ڎ
ڄ ڃ ڇ ڇ ڪ ٺ ٿ ٻ ٻ
(ڻ) ن ڳ ڱ ڦ ٽ ڊ ڏ

English v sometimes is expressed by ۏ .

ARABIC INTEREST TITLES
AVAILABLE
FROM HIPPOCRENE BOOKS

Arabic-English Dictionary
English-Arabic Dictionary
Each volume has approximately 15,000 entries and includes contemporary phrases.
A-E 0487 ISBN 0-7818-0153-2 $14.95 pb
E-A 0519 ISBN 0-7818-0152-4 $14.95 pb

Arabic-English/English-Arabic Learner's Dictionary
Designed for the student, all Arabic words are listed in both the Arabic and Roman scripts. Each volume contains over 18,000 entries.
A-E 0033 ISBN 0-7818-0155-9 $24.95 hc
E-A 0690 ISBN 0-87052-914-5 $14.95 pb

Arabic Grammar for the Written Language
While spoken Arabic varies in different countries, the written language is the same. In just 49 lessons this sterling text will provide the student with a thorough reading knowledge of Arabic as it will be encountered throughout the Moslem world. Keys to all 49 exercises, vocabulary lists, and indexes in both Arabic and English are provided.
1026 ISBN 0-87052-101-2 $19.95pb

Arabic Handy Dictionary
This traveler's companion has a comprehensive English-Arabic section with all the words and phrases listed alphabetically according to the main word in the expression. It's simpler to use than a phrasebook because all the Arabic words and phrases you will meet in stores, on signs and menus, or hear as standard replies are conveniently arranged in subject areas to help you recognize and understand them when they occur.
   The Arabic Handy Dictionary provides practical help with special sections in Arabic-English listed by subject—menu terms, schedules, hotels, streets, etc.—with essential notes on grammar and numbers.
0463 ISBN 0-87052-060-9 $6.95

English-Arabic Conversational Dictionary
This Romanized dictionary is useful in achieving proficiency in the spoken language. The manual contains both the Syrian and Egyptian dialects. Contains over 8,000 entries.
0093 ISBN 0-87052-494-1 $11.95 pb

Mastering Arabic

This imaginative course, designed for both individual and classroom use, assumes no previous knowledge of the language. The unique combination of practical exercises and step-by-step grammar emphasizes a functional approach to new scripts and their vocabularies. Everyday situations and local customs are explored through dialogue, newspaper extracts, drawings, and photos.

Also available is a set of two companion cassettes, totaling 120 minutes of instruction, which follows the lessons in the book and provides listening and pronunciation guidance. This set can be purchased separately or as a book & cassettes package.

0501   ISBN 0-87052-922-6 $14.95pb
0931   ISBN 0-87052-984-6 $12.95cassettes
0110   ISBN 0-87052-984-6 $27.50pb & cassettes

Modern Military Dictionary: English-Arabic/Arabic-English

This timely and necessary dictionary includes fundamental military terms, contemporary political and technological terms and jargon, military technique terms for the specialist, as well as entries for allied subjects such as economics, law, statistics, and sociology.

0947   ISBN 0-87052-987-0 $30.00hc

Arabic for Beginners

Contains concise grammar explanations in each chapter, followed by a vocabulary list and dozens of sentences with translations to reinforce the material. Also includes a "Guide to Arabic Writing," a special 17-page addendum.

0018   ISBN 0-7818-0114-1 $9.95pb

Saudi Arabic Basic Course

Reflecting a preference for "modern" words and structure, this guide will give the student working proficiency in the language to satisfy social demands and business requirements.

0171   ISBN 0-7818-0257-1 $14.95pb

(All prices subject to change.)

TO PURCHASE HIPPOCRENE BOOKS contact your local bookstore, or write to: HIPPOCRENE BOOKS, 171 Madison Avenue, New York, NY 10016. Please enclose check or money order, adding $4.00 shipping (UPS) for the first book and $.50 for each additional book.

THE HIPPOCRENE MASTERING SERIES

MASTERING ARABIC
Jane Wightwick and Mahmoud Gaafar
320 pages • 0-87052-922-6 • $14.95 pb
2 Cassettes 0-87052-984-6 • $12.95
Book & Cassettes 0-87052-140-3 • $27.90

MASTERING FINNISH
Börje Vähämäki
278 pages • 0-7818-0233-4 • $14.95pb
2 Cassettes • 0-78180265-2 • $12.95
Book & Cassettes • 0-7818-0266-0 • $27.90

MASTERING FRENCH
E.J. Neather
288 pages • 0-87052-055-5 • $11.95pb
2 Cassettes • 0-87052-060-1 • $12.95
Book & Cassettes • 0-87052-136-5 • $24.90

MASTERING ADVANCED FRENCH
278 pages • 0-78180312-8 • $11.95pb
2 Cassettes • 0-7818-0313-5 • $12.95
Book & Cassettes • 0-7818-0314-4 • $24.90

MASTERING GERMAN
A.J. Peck
340 pages • 0-87052-056-3 • $11.95 pb
2 Cassettes • 0-87052-061-X • $12.95
Book & Cassettes • 0-87052-137-3 • $24.90

MASTERING ITALIAN
N. Messora
360 pages • 0-87052-057-1 • $11.95 pb
2 Cassettes • 0-87052-066-0 • $12.95
Book & Cassettes • 0-87052-138-1 • $24.90

MASTERING JAPANESE
Harry Guest
368 pages • 0-87052-923-4 • $14.95 pb
2 Cassettes • 0-87052-938-8 • $12.95
Book & Cassettes • 0-87052-141-1 • $27.90

MASTERING POLISH
Albert Juszczak
288 pages • 0-7818-0015-3 • $14.95 pb
2 Cassettes • 0-7818-0016-3 • $12.95
Book & Cassettes • 0-7818-0017-X • $27.90

MASTERING RUSSIAN
Erika Haber
278 pages • 0-7818-0270-9 • $14.95pb
2 Cassettes • 0-7818-0271-7 • $12.95
Book & Cassettes • 0-7818272-5 • $27.90

MASTERING SPANISH
Robert Clarke
338 pages • 0-87052-059-8 • $11.95 pb
2 Cassettes • 0-87052-067-9 • $12.95
Book & Cassettes • 0-87052-139-X • $24.90

MASTERING ADVANCED SPANISH
Robert Clarke
300 pages • 0-7818-0081-1 • $11.95 pb
2 Cassettes • 0-7818-0089-7 • $12.95
Book & Cassettes • 0-7818-0090-0 • $24.90

In praise of the Mastering Series:
• "Truly the best book of its kind."
• "Your book is truly remarkable, and you are to be congratulated."
  —a field editor for college text books.

All prices subject to change.
Ask for these and other Hippocrene titles at your local booksellers!

HIPPOCRENE BEGINNER'S SERIES

Do you know what it takes to make a phone call in Russia? Or how to get through customs in Japan? How about inviting a Czech friend to dinner while visiting Prague? This new language instruction series shows how to handle oneself in typical, day-to-day situations by introducing the business person or traveler not only to the common vocabulary, grammar, and phrases of a new language, but also to the history, customs and daily practices of a foreign country.

The Beginner's Series consists of basic language instruction, which includes vocabulary, grammar, and common phrases and review questions; along with cultural insights, interesting historical background, the country's basic facts, and hints about everyday living—driving, shopping, eating out, making phone calls, extending and accepting an invitation and much more.

Each Guide is 250 pages, 5 1/2 x 8 1/2

BEGINNER'S ROMANIAN

This is a guide designed by **Eurolingua**, the company established in 1990 to meet the growing demand for Eastern European language and cultural instruction. The institute is developing books for business and leisure travelers to all Eastern European countries. This Romanian is a one-of-a-kind for those seeking communication in this newly independent country.

0-7818-0208-3 (0079)
$7.95 paper

BEGINNER'S HUNGARIAN

For the businessman traveling to Budapest, the traveler searching for the perfect spa, or the Hungarian-American searching to extend his or her roots, this guide by **Eurolingua** will aide anyone searching for the words to express basic needs.

0-7818-0209-1 (0068)
$7.95 paper

BEGINNER'S CZECH

The city of Prague has become a major tour destination for Americans who are now often chosing to stay. Here is a guide to the complex language spoken by the natives in an easy to learn format with a guide to phonetics. Also, important Czech history is outlined with cultural notes. This is another guide designed by Eurolingua.

0-7818-0231-8 (0074)
$9.95

BEGINNER'S RUSSIAN

Eurolingua authors **Nonna Karr** and **Ludmila Rodionova** ease English speakers in the Cyrillic alphabet, then introduce enough language and grammar to get a traveler or businessperson anywhere in the new Russian Republic. This book is a perfect stepping-stone to more complex language learning.

0-7818-0232-6 (0061)
$9.95

BEGINNER'S JAPANESE

Author **Joanne Claypoole** runs a consulting business for Japanese people working in America. She has developed her Beginner's Guide for American businesspeople who work for or with Japanese companies in the U.S. or abroad.

Her book is designed to equip the learner with a solid foundation of Japanese conversation. Also included in the text are introductions to Hiragana, Katakana, and Kanji, the three Japanese writing systems.

0-7818-0234-2 (0053)
$9.95

BEGINNER'S ESPERANTO

As a teacher of foreign languages for over 25 years, **Joseph Conroy** knows the need for people of different languages to communicate on a com-mon ground. Though Esperanto has no parent country or land, it is developing an international society all its own. *Beginner's Esperanto* is an introduction to the basic grammar and vocabulary students will need to express their thoughts in the language.

At the end of each lesson, a set of readings gives the student further practice in Esperanto, a culture section will present information about the language and its speakers, a vocabulary lesson group together all the words which occur in the text, and English translations for conversations allow students to check comprehension. As well, the author provides Esperanto contacts with various organizations throughout the world.

0-7818-0230-X (0051)
$14.95 (400 pages)

(All prices subject to change.)

TO PURCHASE HIPPOCRENE BOOKS contact your local bookstore, or write to: HIPPOCRENE BOOKS, 171 Madison Avenue, New York, NY 10016. Please enclose check or money order, adding $4.00 shipping (UPS) for the first book and $.50 for each additional book.

HIPPOCRENE HANDY
and
EXTRA-HANDY DICTIONARIES

For the traveler of independent spirit and curious mind, this practical series will help you to communicate, not just to get by. Common phrases are conveniently listed through key words. Pronunciation follows each entry and a reference section reviews all major grammar points.

Handy Extras are extra helpful—offering even more words and phrases for students and travelers.

ARABIC
$8.95 • 0-87052-960-9

CHINESE
$6.95 • 0-87052-050-4

CZECH EXTRA
$8.95 • 0-7818-0138-9

DUTCH
$6.95 • 0-87052-049-0

FRENCH
$6.95 • 0-7818-0010-2

GERMAN
$6.95 • 0-7818-0014-5

GREEK
$8.95 • 0-87052-961-7

HUNGARIAN EXTRA
$8.95 • 0-7818-0164-8

ITALIAN
$6.95 • 0-7818-0011-0

JAPANESE
$6.95 • 0-87052-962-5

KOREAN
$8.95 • 0-7818-0082-X

PORTUGUESE
$6.95 • 0-87052-053-9

RUSSIAN
$6.95 • 0-7818-0013-7

SERBO-CROATIAN
$6.95 • 0-87052-051-2

SPANISH
$6.95 • 0-7818-0012-9

SWEDISH
$6.95 • 0-87052-054-7

THAI
$8.95 • 0-87052-963-3

TURKISH
$6.95 • 0-87052-982-X

HIPPOCRENE AFRICAN LANGUAGE LIBRARY

For travelers to Africa, for African-Americans exploring their roots, and for everyone interested in learning more about Africa and her languages, we offer the new African Language Library.

ENGLISH-SOMALI/SOMALI-ENGLISH DICTIONARY
Somali is spoken by 8 million in Africa. Features 11,000 up-to-date entries with clear pronunciation.
276 pages • 5 1/2 x 9 • $29.50 cloth • 0-7818-0269-5

SWAHILI PHRASEBOOK, *T. Gilmore and S. Kwasa*
A straightforward guide to basic communication in many African countries from Botswana in the south to centrally situated Zaire to Kenya and Ethiopia in the east.
184 pages • 4 x 5 3/8 • $8.95 paper • 0-87052-970-6

TWI-ENGLISH/ENGLISH-TWI CONCISE DICTIONARY, *Paul Kotey*
Twi is the major language of Ghana and it is spoken by 6 million people.
Brand new and easy-to-use, this is **the only Twi-English/English-Twi dictionary available in the U.S.** 8,000 entries accompanied by common-sense phonetics.
425 pages • 3 5/8 x 5 3/8 • $11.95 paper • 0-7818-0264-4

A NEW CONCISE XHOSA-ENGLISH DICTIONARY, *J. McLaren*
One of the Bantu languages, Xhosa is spoken by about 4 million people. A standard among students of Xhosa since 1914, this edition of *A New Concise Xhosa-English Dictionary* contains approximately 6,000 modern entries and an extensive section on pronunciation, emphasizing the distinct Xhosa tone and accent.
194 pages • 4 3/4 x 7 1/8 • $14.95 paper • 0-7818-0251-2

YORUBA-ENGLISH/ ENGLISH-YORUBA CONCISE DICTIONARY, *Olabiyi Yai*
One of the major languages of Nigeria, Yoruba is spoken by 15 million people. **The only Yoruba-English/English-Yoruba dictionary to be offered in the U.S.**, this concise reference provides a thorough grounding in vocabulary and emphasizes the rise and fall of the voice, essential to speaking this beautiful tongue.
375 pages • 3 5/8 x 5 3/8 • $11.95 paper • 0-7818-0263-6

ZULU-ENGLISH/ENGLISH-ZULU DICTIONARY, *G.R. Dent and C.L.S. Nyembezi*
Zulu is one of the major Bantu languages of South Africa, originating in the easternmost part of the country. Over 4 million people speak Zulu.
With 30,000 updated and modern entries, most with multiple definitions, this dictionary is one of the most comprehensive Zulu-English dictionaries available anywhere.
519 pages • 7 1/4 x 4 3/4 • $29.50 paper • 0-7818-0255-5

Companion Guide to Saudi Arabia

by Gene Lindsey

For travelers to Saudi Arabia (especially women), or for students of the Arabic culture, this guide helps a western thinker understand the intense conflicts that have slowly drawn U.S. military and business interests to the area.

In his fascinating book, Gene Lindsey, an American businessman who spent much of the 1980s in Saudi Arabia, traces the history of the region, its religion, its Bedoin heritage, its rags-to-riches development, the harsh environment, foreign policy, its laws, language, education, technology, its way of doing business, and underlying it all its mindset.

The book also contains one topographical map, and three political maps of the Arabian Peninsula.

368 pages with bibliography and index
$11.95 paperback
0-7818-0023-4

LIGHTNING IN THE STORM
The 101st Air Assault Division in the Gulf War
Thomas Taylor

As the only air assault division in the world, the 101st Airborne Division—the Screaming Eagles—flew off to Saudi Arabia to join the Desert Shield; 18,000 soldiers, including 700 women, and 400 helicopters—Apaches, Cobras, Kiowas, Black Hawks, and Chinooks—to play a crucial role in Desert Storm. This is their story, told by Thomas Taylor (who served with the Screaming Eagles in Vietnam), who interviewed hundreds of them.

The Gulf War was their rendezvous with destiny; superbly trained and led by America's finest officers, uniquely qualified for the task at hand, tested by cruel destiny—248 deaths in an airplane crash at Gander in 1985—the 101st performed two major tasks in the war: the assault on Iraqi's radar which "plucked its eyes" in Gen. Schwarzkopf's phrase, and the cutting off of Iraq's main supply route from Baghdad to the forces in Kuwait.

Thunderous Praise for Lightning in the Storm:

"*Lightning in the Storm* establishes Thomas Taylor as one of America's foremost military historians. This exceptionally well-written battlefield account of the 101st Air Assault Division's role in the decisive "Hail Mary" air/land strike in the Gulf War, is brought alive by Taylor's personal experience in combat and his visceral understanding of fighting men. Required reading for anyone interested in the contemporary American military." —Al Santoli, author of *Leading the Way: How Vietnam Veterans Rebuilt the U.S. Military*

"Beyond entertainment and excitement, Thomas Taylor has put together the kind of account future historians will find must reading....Superbly detailed and written." • —John DelVecchio, author of *The 13th Valley* and a former Screaming Eagle

MILITARY BOOK CLUB MAIN SELECTION

Thomas H. Taylor is a highly decorated combat veteran of the 101st, who had exclusive access to the division's Gulf War journals, photo files, and video tape. After practicing law in Saudi Arabia, Taylor turned to writing full time. Retired from the U.S. Army Reserves as a colonel in 1991, Taylor has authored five books and presently lives in Washington, D.C.

468 pages, 47 b/w photos, 12 charts & maps
$29.50 hc • 0-7818-0268-7

ADDITIONAL DICTIONARIES FROM HIPPOCRENE...